# ALONG THE OLD YORK ROAD

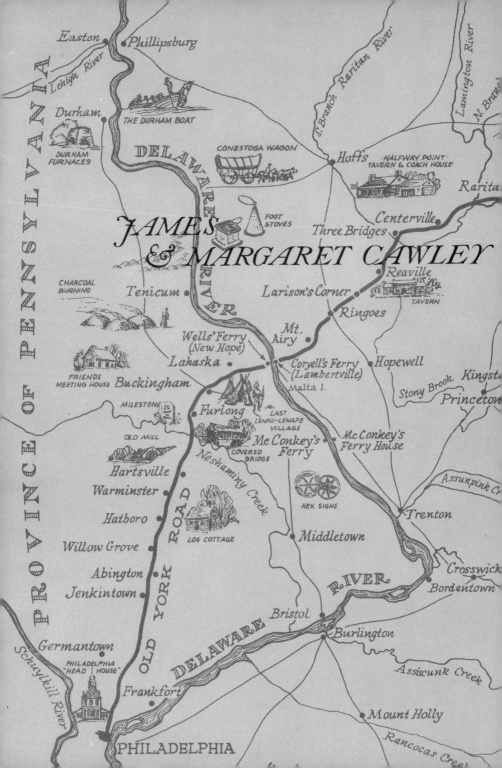

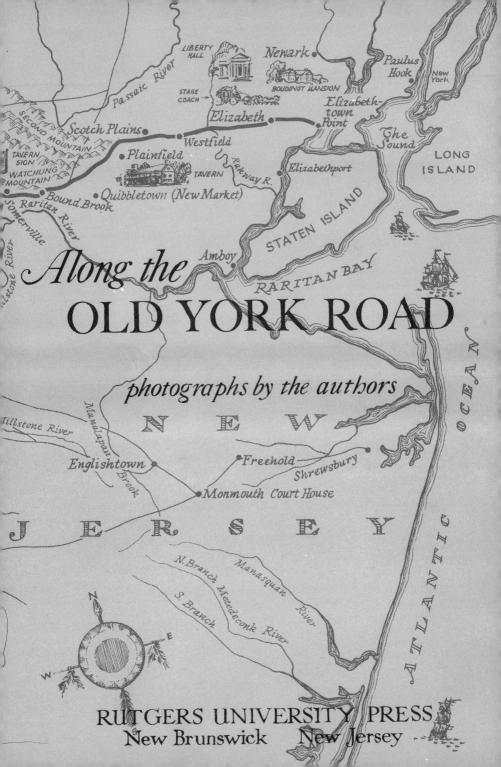

# Along the OLD YORK ROAD

*photographs by the authors*

RUTGERS UNIVERSITY PRESS
New Brunswick • New Jersey

*Library of Congress Catalogue Card Number: 65-19397*
*SBN: 8135-0487-2*

*Manufactured in the United States of America by*
*Quinn & Boden Company, Inc., Rahway, New Jersey*

*The authors are grateful for permission to quote in this volume passages from* The Delaware, *by Harry Emerson Wildes, published by Holt, Rinehart and Winston, Inc.*

For our ten grandchildren: Donald, James, Stephen, Edward, Jeff, Jennifer, Susan, Katherine, Jane, Kathleen, in the hope that they will always share our love and appreciation of their American Heritage.

# PREFACE

The New Jersey portion of the Old York Road has always fascinated me. I remember it when, as a small boy, I was allowed to accompany my Dad on his inspection trips over the "long lines" of the telephone company that ran beside the road. We traveled by horse and buggy, and the journeys took all day. The quiet countryside, beautiful scenery, and the soft plodding of the horse's hooves in the thick dust of the road are still sharp in my mind.

I have a still greater personal identification with the old stage road, as my maternal ancestor, Peter Fisher, settled in 1729 on a 200-acre farm beside a trail that was later to become the Old York Road, near Ringoes. His original log cabin has long since disappeared, but the farmhouse he built twelve years later is standing. Carved in a stone of one of the fireplaces may still be seen his initials, P. F., and the date, 1741. I am a sixth generation descendent. The farm is now owned by my good friends, Mr. and Mrs. Kenneth Heston, who maintain it in perfect condition.

The York Road, or the Old York Road, as it came to be known in later years, was considered one of the most important of the few roads that existed in late Colonial and early Federal years, mainly because it was the shortest and fastest overland route between New York and Philadelphia. Thus our road not only played an important part in the development of commerce between the two cities; it also became the main travel artery across New Jersey, to which feeder roads were later built. The road was of great strategic value to the Continental Army during the Revolutionary War for the movement of men and supplies.

Our road is today a busy modern highway of blacktop and concrete and the high-crowned road of yesteryear is no more. But one may still savor its charm. On many parts of it there is the same beautiful countryside, and a surprising number of the buildings erected in Colonial days still stand.

The reader who will spend a day or so exploring the Old York Road by car, stopping for a time in some of the villages, particularly west of the Raritan, will find his journey richly rewarding.

JAMES S. CAWLEY, co-author

April, 1965

# CONTENTS

# The Early Years of the Old York Road

A replica of one of the more elaborate private coaches used on the stage roads of the Colonies. This picture was made at Palmer Square in Princeton during a celebration of the one-hundred-and-fiftieth anniversary of George Washington's journey from Mount Vernon to New York City for his inauguration as first President of the United States.

*There is in history no agency so wondrous, no working in-strumentality so great, as transportation.*—EMERSON HOUGH

The earliest highways in the American Colonies were In-dian paths and the bays and rivers over which the Indians had been paddling canoes and dugouts for centuries. In 1664, the year in which New Jersey acquired its name and became a separate province, there were few roads of any length in this colony or in Pennsylvania, its neighbor across the Delaware. There was Lawrie's or the "Lower Road," from Burlington to the ferry at Amboy; another was the "Old Dutch Road," built originally over the Assanpink Trail from Elizabethtown through Woodbridge, Piscataway, and Inian's Ferry (New Brunswick) down to the Delaware where Trenton now is. A road also followed the north bank of the Raritan through Bound Brook, Raritan, and west to "The Forks," where the north and south branches of the river meet.

The first road of all, and probably the oldest commercial wheeled-vehicle road in the country, was the Old Mine Road, built by Dutch settlers in the early seventeenth cen-tury. The Old Mine Road ran from Esopus (now Kingston, N.Y.) on the Hudson River west to the Delaware River and south to the Water Gap, where copper mines at Pahaquarry had been worked by the Indians for unknown

SITE OF
LANDING OF
CAPTAIN PHILIP de CARTERET
1665
First Royal Governor
of the Colony of New Jersey

Marker at the eastern terminus of the Old York Road. Here, at the foot of present-day Elizabeth Avenue, stage passengers boarded the ferry for the Battery in Manhattan.

years. Records of this road are scanty, but we do know that it was built by the Dutch because the Indians had no wheeled vehicles. Copper utensils thought to be made from ore from the Pahaquarry mines are in museums in Holland.

The York Road, the subject of this volume, had one characteristic that distinguished it from other colonial roads— it was built from west to east, to connect Philadelphia to New York.

The Pennsylvania section of the Old York Road had been cleared and roughly graded by about 1725, but for many years it was still too rough for vehicle travel. The whole of the road across New Jersey from Coryell's Ferry (Lambertville) to Elizabethtown Point was not open for vehicle traffic until 1764. Most of it did, however, exist in a series of local roads, trails, or paths from one settlement to another. The York Road in the Province of Pennsylvania appeared on a map published in Philadelphia by Nicholas Scull in 1759.

It is difficult, in these fast-moving times, to realize the physical conditions in the Colonies during the seventeenth century. Few of the colonists knew any region other than the coastal areas where the first settlements were founded.

As more immigrants came to the New World, the shore settlements seemed crowded to some of the more adventurous colonists, and they began to penetrate the interior lands. They had to travel over the Indian paths or make their way up the rivers. Some of them journeyed to the upper reaches of the Delaware and Schuylkill Rivers, using the birch-bark canoes and dugouts they had adopted from the Indians. Such streams afforded an easier method of travel than did the paths over which they could walk or ride a horse. It was not, however, until large grants of land were made to Wil-

Presbyterian Church in Westfield, near the site of the original church
built in 1735.

liam Penn and Lords Carteret and Berkeley that any real effort was made to settle inland.

Penn's "Holy Experiment," following the acquisition of a substantial part of the Pennsylvania Colony in the "Walking Purchase," was the beginning of the settlement of that area. The land was heavily forested, and there were as yet no roads.

Historians are still debating what the actual arrangements with the Indians were for the "Walking Purchase." It would appear that the whole deal was something of a sharp real estate transaction, much like some of those consummated today. Thomas Penn, the son of William, made the deal with the Delaware chiefs who claimed they owned all the land along the Delaware River. The Six Nations Indian Federation argued that the Delawares had no more land to sell and that they could not therefore agree to the "Walking Purchase." To convince the Delawares that they (the Indians) were obligated to the Quaker colony, Thomas Penn showed the chiefs a "deed" which he (Thomas) claimed had been given in 1686 to his father, whom the Indians highly respected. In the so-called "deed" it had been agreed between the Indians and William Penn that Penn was to have "all the land a man can walk over in a day and a half." The authenticity of the document is doubtful, but Thomas finally convinced the Indians that they should honor it. Accordingly, arrangements were made to conduct the walkabout in the fall of 1737, shortly after the completion of the York Road from Philadelphia to Wells' Ferry.

There was a wide divergence of opinion between the Indians and the settlers as to what had been agreed upon in the "deed." The Indians interpreted it to mean a leisurely

7

walk, pausing for refreshments and ending the walk at sundown. In fact, what the Indians had in mind was a distance of about thirty-five miles along the Delaware River to a point where Easton is now located.

Thomas Penn had other ideas. He found three of the best young athletes in the Colony and told them to go into training and to familiarize themselves with the area to be walked over. They were told to blaze a trail so that no time would be lost when the actual "walk" began. An added inducement was the promise of five pounds in money and five hundred acres of land to the man who covered the greatest distance.

On the great day a group of Indians and white settlers met at the starting point. Penn's experts walked at a quick

Scotch Plains Tavern. The center section was built in 1737, and except for a few years when it was a private residence, has been continuously in use as a tavern.

pace, actually a half lope, until the Indians were outdistanced. Then, it is said, horses were furnished to the white walkers, and riding a considerable distance on horseback, they left the Indians far behind. Even so, only one of the white men stayed in the race. He was Edward Marshall, and at the end of a day and a half Marshall had covered sixty-six miles, to a point near present-day Jim Thorpe, formerly the town of Mauch Chunk.

The Indians realized that they had been outsmarted but kept their agreement with Thomas Penn. In 1758, Penn gave the Six Nations the northern half of the purchase and the Colony paid the Delawares four hundred pounds for the southern portion. Thus, much of what is now Eastern Pennsylvania was bought by the Quaker Colony for about a shilling, or its equivalent, an acre.

Because of the difficulty of travel most of the settlers who bought land tracts in the interior had to journey to their new locations over the Indian paths, with only such goods as could be carried on their backs or on the horses, oxen, and cows, if they were lucky enough to have such animals. Strong backs, axes, and seeds for the first crops were the essentials.

As soon as the land was taken up the first task confronting the new settlers in the interior was the backbreaking job of clearing the land of the virgin timber, with which it was heavily forested except for some meadow areas along the rivers. The trees, usually stands of pine, hemlock, and hardwoods were difficult to cut with the simple tools the settlers used. As a rule the cut timber that was not used for the cabins, other farm buildings, and fences was piled and burned in the winter, when it was safe to do so. The burning of the timber made huge quantities of wood ashes, and this was the beginning of a new industry, the making of potash. The settlers ran water through the ashes and evaporated the lye in iron pots. The resulting product was boiled with fats to make the crude soap of the day. Potash was in great demand, not only in the Colonies but in Europe, and all that could be transported to the coast could be sold.

Once the land had been cleared, the seeds for the first crop were sown around the tree stumps. Later the stumps were burned and pulled out, and eventually large areas of land were cleared for cultivation.

The first job after arriving at the land holding was of course the building of a shelter for the family. Trees were selected and cut for the building of a cabin. Other farm buildings such as open shelters and later closed storage barns had to wait a while. In many cases the first cabins were later incorporated into the more pretentious farmhouses as kitchen lean-tos. The building of a springhouse, at first of logs and later of stone if it was available, was an immediate requirement to keep meat, butter, and other perishables. Those stone springhouses may still be found on some of the older farms in New Jersey and in Pennsylvania. In fact, many are still being used, despite the general availability of modern refrigeration.

Before roads were constructed throughout the Provinces of New Jersey and Pennsylvania the larger rivers, particularly the Schuylkill and the Delaware, played an important part in getting goods to market. As the white settlers wanted to carry larger cargoes than could be handled in the canoes and dugouts of the Indians, larger boats were built. The most famous of these early cargo carriers were the Durham boats, developed to travel through the fast white water, particularly in the Delaware. The Delaware bateau, a shallow-draft, barge-type craft was also used to carry cargo.

A Durham boat being poled through ice floes on the Delaware. (*Reproduced from a drawing, courtesy of the Standard Pressed Steel Co.*)

The very early settlers who took land in the open reaches of the Delaware valley were more fortunate than those who settled the interior in having a ready-to-use-highway—the rivers. It was the practice for years to store the farm crops in community storehouses such as Holcombe's at Mount Airy, New Jersey, until they could be carted to the river during the spring high water and floated down to the Philadelphia and other coastal markets. The Raritan River was also used in this manner by the early Dutch settlers to get their grain and other farm products to tidewater at Landing Bridge, above what is now New Brunswick. The Durham boats were not used on the shallower Raritan. Rough flat boats carried the cargo downstream with the current, and as there were no deep rapids, the craft could be poled back to the mills or farms.

The Holcombe storehouse at Mount Airy.

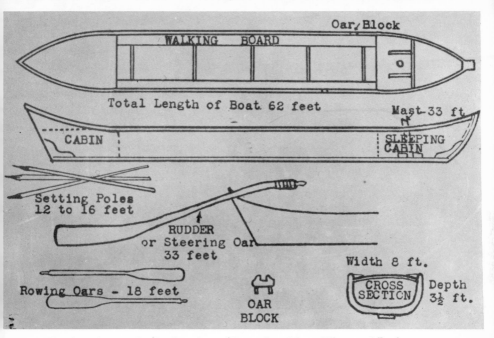

Working plans of the Durham boat. (*Reproduced from* History of Bucks County, Pennsylvania, *by W. W. Davis.*)

The Delaware in those early days was a deeper and rougher stream than it is now. Cutting the forest cover in its watershed and the use of water from the Delaware and its tributaries have reduced the volume of flow to a fraction of what it was two hundred years ago. It is probable that had not such a craft as the Durham boat been available to early settlers, the upper reaches of the Delaware and the Schuylkill would not have been settled until much later.

The Durham boat represented the first major advance in commercial transportation in the Colonies, paralleling but somewhat antedating the various kinds of cargo wagons that were developed as roads became usable for wheeled vehicles. Robert Durham began about 1750 to build these keel-boats, shaped like an Indian bark canoe, at his iron furnace near

13

Easton, Pennsylvania. They varied in size, the largest being sixty-six feet long, and carrying fifteen tons, and by the time of the Revolution there were so many of them along the river that they were the boats George Washington's men secretly collected for the famous crossing of the Delaware.

Successfully piloting such a boat, loaded with its cargo and crew, through the rapids called for expert handling. Of course the heavy cargoes were transported only during the time of high water. Even in those days the normal state of the water would not permit such commerce. The boats were of shallow draft and slightly rockered for quick maneuverability. A huge sweep was used at the stern for steering and along each side were hinged walkways for the crew to use while poling the boat. Those same walkways could be turned up and used as splashboards while running the rapids. A single mast was stepped forward for the sail when wind and water conditions permitted its use on the return journeys upriver. On the downstream trips local pilots were employed at some of the worst rapids. The fee for such a job was usually five dollars.

The return journeys did not require so much skill as plain brawn. At some of the rapids such as Wells' Falls, where there was and still is, a fourteen-foot drop in three-quarters of a mile, and at Fowl Rift near Belvidere, ring bolts were fastened on the rocks and the walls of the cliffs, to which ropes were attached to haul the boats upstream.

The Durham boats were used for a hundred years or more, and were gradually abandoned only after the building of canals in the nineteenth century. The last man known to have taken a cargo down the river in a Durham boat was William Lagar of Lumberville, Pennsylvania, in 1865.

So far as the authors could discover, not one original Durham boat remains today. There is a half-scale replica on display at St. John Terrell's Music Circus at Lambertville, built from the old plans by local boatwrights. Once a year, on Christmas Day, Mr. Terrell and a group of his friends, dressed in Continental Army uniforms, use this boat to re-enact George Washington's crossing of the Delaware.

The settlers on the rivers had easy access to the markets, using the rivers as their highways, but those in the interior were not so fortunate. They had used the Indian paths to get to their new land holdings and they continued to use them. These paths were well laid out and were easy to travel on foot or horseback but wheeled vehicles to take cargoes to market could not use them. The Indian paths, as the early settlers learned, were carefully planned to take advantage of the best routes to travel. The hills were ascended by the easiest grades; the solid ground instead of marshy areas was selected for the fords to avoid places that would be flooded during the spring freshets. It was such paths which were later widened to become early roads like the York Road.

As more land was cleared and planted, a need arose for mills to grind the grains and grist mills were built on streams with sufficient water flow to turn the wheels. To get the grain to the nearest mill the settlers hacked out rough "ways" from their farms to the mill. It was natural that as traffic increased other enterprises should be built around the mills—stores, taverns, a smithy, and other ventures to sell and trade with the farmers as they waited for their grain to be ground. Thus many of our present-day communities had their beginnings.

Tucca-Ramma-Hacking, "meeting place of the waters," where the North and South Branches of the Raritan come together.

Originally the farms produced only enough for family consumption, but as time went on, they began to have surpluses. A ready market existed in the coastal towns, if the farmers could get their wagonloads of produce to them.

As the settlers in both provinces felt the increasing need for land transportation, efforts were started to get their provincial officials to build roads. The Colonial governors responded by appointing commissioners to study and survey the best routes.

In the Jerseys, the first official step in this direction was the appointment, in 1675, of two men to "lay out common highways." In March, 1683, a commission was created to "lay out and appoint" in the several counties, "all necessary highways, bridges, passages, landings, and ferries, fit and apt for traveling, passages, and landing of goods." These boards continued for a number of years, thus laying the foundation for New Jersey's present highway system. No appropriation of money, however, went along with the appointment. The actual expense, which was mostly labor, was then, and for many years thereafter, considered a local responsibility.

In Pennsylvania, the petition of the Cheltenham Township settlers to the royal governor in 1693 was the first step in the building of roads in that province. This was followed in 1711 by the appointment of commissioners to survey the possibility of widening the Lenni-Lenape path from Philadelphia north to the Delaware at what is now Center Bridge. However, when it was determined that a shorter and better route would run directly from what is now Lahaska, on the original road, to Wells' Ferry on the Delaware, a new portion of the road was built and this later became the through stage route.

It was more than thirty years before the road was completed across the Provinces of the Jerseys to Elizabethtown Point. In the building of the Jersey portion of the road many stretches of existing roads and "ways," like the "King's Highway" and the River Road along the Raritan from "The Forks" were linked together. In a deed made at Ringoes dated August 25, 1726, reference is made to "the King's Highway that is called the York Road," which would indicate that the through road was completed at least to that point. However, it was not until 1764 that a survey of the road was made across Somerset County.

John Holcombe, who owned several thousand acres of land along the Delaware on the Jersey side, including what is now Lambertville, wanted the Jersey part of the road

Stone bridge on the "King's Highway" at Bound Brook, built some time before 1700. The brook which it formerly spanned has been channeled aside. At the center of the bridge is the boundary between Somerset and Middlesex Counties, the eastern terminus of Somerset County's York Road Survey of 1764.

built over his land. John Reading, a man of equal wealth, owned a ferry a few miles up the river at what is now Stockton. He, too, wanted the road to cross at his ferry and continue over his land, and he had enough influence to cause the Pennsylvania Commissioners to lay out the road to his ferry at what is now Center Bridge. Holcombe finally won out and the Jersey part of the road eventually continued over his land.

While the "Upper Road" from Lahaska did not become part of the through route to New York, it did enable local settlers along its route to get to the Philadelphia and coastal markets. The main road from Philadelphia to Wells' Ferry then became known as the "Lower Road." A few years before this controversy, John Wells had obtained a seven-year lease from the Colonial Governors of Pennsylvania to operate his ferry. He paid an annual rental of forty shillings, which gave him exclusive rights to run a ferry within the distance of four miles along the river.

The Pennsylvania Road Commissioners were wise in their planning, envisioning as they did the future needs of the Province for more and better land transportation. In New Jersey, there was the same awareness of the problem, as William Franklin, the last Royal Governor of New Jersey said in his message to the legislature in 1768, "Even those roads which lie between the two chief trading cities in America, are seldom passable without danger or difficulty."

The Cornell mansion at Raritan. Section on the right was built as a tavern by George Middagh in 1734.

So, having recognized the importance of New York and Philadelphia as commercial centers and of more and better roads as the key to economic growth, road building and improvement was stepped up in the two neighboring colonies. In eastern Pennsylvania the roads, for the most part, were planned to connect the greatest number of interior settlements with Philadelphia and other larger centers. In the Jersey provinces the big markets were to the eastward: Elizabethtown, Newark, Amboy, and a few other communities.

With little if any road-building funds, labor had to be supplied by the farmers living along the routes. When the New Jersey townships were incorporated in 1798, local road officials were appointed and some funds became available. However, the farmers were still responsible not only for most of the labor in constructing roads, but in maintaining them. They were able in this way to work out all or part of their taxes.

The early road specifications called for a minimum width of forty feet, and there was some attempt to adhere to this rule. In practice, however, only a vehicle width in the center was properly graded. The farmers found that too much of their time was required, particularly during the planting and harvest seasons, to maintain their sections of the roads. To lessen their work many of them moved their fences in toward the center of the road, little by little, until only the graded center was left, leaving about half the original width.

In the spring those early roads, including the York Road, were all but impassable and a journey of any length was avoided unless it was absolutely necessary. This situation, together with the winter snows, left only a few months

The Naraticong Trail marker on the Old York Road at Raritan.

during the year when the roads could be used by vehicles. Man on horseback fared much better.

When the York Road was completed across the Jersey provinces by way of Mount Airy, from the ferry, and on to Ringoes, Reaville, Three Bridges, Centerville, Raritan, part of which is now Somerville, Bound Brook, New Market, Plainfield, Scotch Plains, Westfield, Garwood, and Elizabethtown Point ferry, a vehicle road now existed over the shortest distance between Philadelphia and the Elizabethtown ferry. Vehicle traffic was possible over the portion of the road that crossed the Jerseys as soon as it was completed in 1764. Unlike the earlier portion of the road in Pennsylvania, the Jersey section utilized large stretches of roads already existing

21

and many of the old streets and roads between communities were incorporated into the through road.

During the latter part of the eighteenth century and much of the nineteenth, the increasing need for building and boat timber resulted in the spectacular rafting era on the Delaware River. Uncut timber was plentiful all over the provinces but the existing roads were not of a nature that would permit the cartage of the timber to Philadelphia and other centers where there were mills to cut the logs into finished lumber. A natural highway already existed—the river down which the timber could be floated in the form of large rafts.

The authors have over many years spent a lot of time canoe cruising the entire length of the Delaware and during those years have heard many and sometimes wondrous stories

Shohola, one of the rapids in the Delaware.

from old timers on the river. We were fortunate to have become acquainted with the upper river early enough to have talked to many men who had participated in the rafting runs and so much of our information is at first hand.

Like spectacular exploits everywhere, the stories got bigger over the years and perhaps also with the touches we ourselves have added to them it is sometimes difficult to separate legends from facts.

The great forests of the Catskills provided material for log rafts, some of which were over eighty feet long. To get such cumbersome affairs through the many rapids of the river required special hardiness and navigating skill.

The lumber used in the building of the Fisher farmhouse, mentioned in the preface to this volume, was rafted down-river to Coryell's Ferry and carted overland to the farm. Incidentally, the total cost of the materials for this large house came to about eight hundred dollars.

There are hundreds of stories, legends, and traditions about the rafting days. One of the more vivid descriptions is contained in Harry Emerson Wildes' book, *The Delaware*, one of the Rivers of America series:

"Britain's naval needs first led to a full use of the river. Shipbuilders on the lower Delaware, making brigs and sloops and small three-masted snows for the West Indian trade, offered markets for the loggers of the Catskills and for the husky raftsmen who floated the timber downstream to the Philadelphia yards. Lumber, therefore, was the first great industry to unify the people of the Delaware, and to bind all the settlers on the stream into a cooperative common-wealth. . . .

"The raftsmen were brawny rivermen, powerful with their huge sweeps, wise in their knowledge of the shifting channels.

23

Long before the Revolution had begun, shrewd Dan Skinner, admiral of the raft fleet, and Josiah Parks, his obstreperous bosun, were rafting eighty-foot pine logs from the Catskill foothills down to Philadelphia and walking back upstream through the untracked forests, with their pockets full of gold. . . .

"Each raft, before it entered the U-turn at Peas Island, tied up to receive its store of rum sufficient to make each raftsman drunk. Then, sending his happy men forward through the danger zone, where they would pole and push the logs, often while wading in cold water up to the waist and shoulders, Dan Skinner prepared a second rum supply to greet them after they emerged. Each raftsman knew that Peas Island was a place for heavy labor, but he knew also that Peas Island was the spot where he would get drunk twice. Instead of shirking the hard work, he looked forward to the crisis with gleeful anticipation. . . .

"Below Hancock, the raftsman's job was somewhat less exacting. . . . Dan Skinner's men were under orders to tie up for the night, liquorless, that they might start next morning, fresh and rested, for the passage of Long Eddy, for the swift run about Conchecton Hill, and for the passage through the Dreamer Islands, where rafts were almost sure to ground. Once past these danger spots, once south of "Lackawack," where the rapid Lackawaxen River flows into the Delaware, once over the dreaded Minisink ford, where whirlpools swung many a raft onto the rocks, carousing was allowed, to celebrate the safe voyage. The inns that lay below the Lackawack and Minisink were noisy with the songs and boasts and riotings of raftsmen."

All of the rapids mentioned in the account of the rafting days are familiar to the authors, who have run them many times in a canoe. This has been a favorite form of recreation for that peculiar breed of men and women known as cruising canoeists, and in our family it is of three generations' duration. Members of the Atlantic Division of the American Canoe Association, the Murray Hill Canoe Club, and others are still cruising the river during the spring season of higher water. Perhaps one could truthfully say that these generations have been of as hardy a breed as the raftsmen of old. Certainly the heavy white water looms much higher and more dangerous from a sixteen-foot canoe than it did from the deck of an eighty-foot raft.

As these passages are written, the authors are planning a Delaware cruise for the coming weekend. It is fall and the water will probably be cold, but the thrill of the cruise is just as great, in anticipation, as it was a half-century ago.

The Delaware River was the Elysium of the Indian tribes that inhabited its shores. Even today sites of their villages are being uncovered. The Trenton Museum doubtless has one of the finest collections of artifacts from excavations along the river that can be found anywhere. A chance find like the one near Kintnersville where a bulldozer turned over several skeletons is the manner in which many village sites are located. The authors had the privilege of working in one such "dig."

The white man, as did the Indians for centuries before him, came to love the Delaware valley, and, over the years, many legends, stories, and poems have been written about life along the river. One, "The Ode to The Delaware," by an unknown author, described the river in this manner in 1893:

> All powerful and restless,
> On it flows to meet the ocean

Flows the historic Delaware.
Not a jot its restless motion,
Shore, or rocks, or islets, spare.
As the untutored child of nature,
Down its rock-barred course wild
Forms it here an isle or rift:
Yet at times 'tis peaceful, mild
Still thou floweth on, resistless.
Flowing in, and out, and onward,
Ever gaining strength and force
As the fall, which rushing downward,
Swells thy torrent in its course.

Let us leave the rivers that were important when roads
were few and far between, and go back to the third quarter
of the eighteenth century. By then the provinces of both the
Jerseys and of Pennsylvania finally had a through vehicle
road from Philadelphia to Elizabethtown and Newark, with
ferry connections at both ends. The first part of the road,
from Philadelphia to Wells' Ferry, was not used to any
extent by any kind of vehicles, except perhaps the heavy
farm carts and wagons, until near the middle of the eighteenth century. The Pennsylvania part of the highway was
newly constructed and, unlike the Jersey part, there were no
existing thoroughfares to incorporate into the thirty miles
of road. The removal of stumps and boulders left holes to
be filled with dirt and they became mud holes during the
rainy season. In fact, some of the places were so bad that
split tree trunks had to be laid over the mud areas to prevent the vehicles from sinking to their hubs. At times the
difficulty of travel made passage over the roads, except on
foot or horseback, prohibitive until the mud dried.

All early roads were dusty in dry and muddy in wet seasons. By breaking the surface of the road at intervals with cross ditches on the steeper pitches, washouts were checked to a degree. Those ditches were known as "thank-you-ma'ams" and in addition to preventing erosion they served as brakes to hold the vehicles while the horses took a breather.

Today's motorist, traveling over these same roads in a comfortable car and driving from Philadelphia to New York in a matter of hours instead of days, finds it difficult to realize the discomfort and downright hardship of road travel in those days. Of course the passengers on the early stage wagons sometimes complained, or should we say usually complained, about the hardships of the road, but on the whole they accepted conditions as the lesser of two evils. They had two other choices—walking or riding on horseback. Actually, the so-called stages, during the early years of the stage lines, were not like the relatively comfortable and sometimes elaborate Concord coaches used after the Revolution. They were simply farm wagons with two or three crossboards for seats. For protection from the weather there was a canvas top fitted over bows. Those hard-riding vehicles could carry up to a dozen people, who had to sit on the crossbenches and usually hang on for dear life when the going got rough, which was most of the time.

As stage travel became more popular, some effort was made to provide more comfort for the passengers. Not much could be done in that direction as the wagons had no springs and the wagon body was affixed to the axles. With the invention of the elliptical spring about 1820 some of the stages were fitted with them. Still later, when metal springs were available, it was a bit more comfortable to ride in the stages.

As competition among stage lines became greater, such

luxuries as straw-filled cushions for the hard board seats were added. However, none of those early stage wagons could be described as being comfortable to any degree.

Most of the stage drivers were arrogant and couldn't care less about the comfort of their passengers. To hold to their schedules was the main consideration and whether the customers were jolted unmercifully apparently was no concern of the driver. Doubtless the increased competition for business later changed that attitude to some degree.

Reverting for a moment to the bottomless mud holes so frequently encountered during the spring rainy season on the York Road, there was a story told and retold by the stage drivers whenever they could find someone credulous enough to believe it: "While driving along I saw a man's hat in the middle of the road and I called out to know who was there. Answer from the mud, 'It's me! but take no thought about me; there's a man a-horse-back below me and he can't get out.'" With the established routine of a two-day journey by stage between New York and Philadelphia, the road became better graded and maintained. Traffic moved faster and it became the exception, rather than the rule, for vehicles to be delayed for road repairs.

From all accounts about the early days of the Old York Road it would appear that from the day it opened, particularly in the Jersey provinces, the road became a popular route for travel by an ever-increasing number of people. In fact, it is said that at one time as many as two hundred vehicles passed over the road in a single day. Considering the smaller population along the eastern seaboard at that time, the road would seem to have been as relatively popular as our present-day highways.

Frequent stops to change horses and the mid-day meals

The original tavern barn at Centerville, now used as a community house.

gave passengers a chance to get out and walk the cramps out of their legs. Farmers made no complaints about the condition of the roads, as their growing number made possible weekly journeys to larger markets and a chance to shop and trade.

During the first third of the nineteenth century, private turnpike companies were chartered and many toll roads were constructed, in some cases near existing roads, but also in places where no road had been built by the townships. Through the sale of stock and the collection of tolls a good return resulted from many of those operations. Unlike today, the tolls were low and as a rule the toll collectors were families who lived at the tollgates. A long pole, similar to the old-time well sweeps, extended across the road and, when the toll was paid, the pole was raised to allow the vehicle, people, or cattle to pass through. Toll was charged for horseback riders and there was a head charge on cattle and sheep.

Many people still living remember the last of the tollgates. Some were still in operation as late as fifty years ago. Here and there some of the former tollhouses may still be seen along the highways.

As is sometimes the case today, people objected to paying tolls and there were all sorts of schemes thought up to avoid them. One of the most popular was the building of detours, or "shunpikes" as they were known, around the tollgates. Sometimes the farmer who permitted the use of his fields for this purpose would himself later charge tolls.

After the Revolution the more elaborate Concord coaches, that up to that time had only been seen in the larger cities, were put on the road as stagecoaches. Padded seats and strap suspension made them elegant compared to the crude stage wagons. Some of them were very colorful and had the name of the stage line painted on each side. Many were in reality as large as tally-ho coaches, usually drawn by four and sometimes six horses, with a gaily uniformed driver on the box.

The years following the Revolutionary War showed a great increase in the number of stage lines operating. Their many vehicles, together with the long processions of Jersey wagons, Conestogas, and others could be seen going to and fro daily. On certain days of the week, it is said, some vehicle was always in sight throughout the length of the stage highway.

Freighting by wagons was an important method of exchange of products with other areas. Long lines of wagons carried great loads of farm produce. They were the equivalent of our modern diesel rigs. It is true, however, that much

Ringoes Tavern, built in 1840.

of the freight destined for coastal cities was still carried in sailing ships.

The outstanding stage coaches on the Old York Road were those of the Swift-Sure Stage Line. In 1769 advertisements appearing in the *New York Gazette or Weekly Post Boy* announced: "A new stage line is to be erected to go from New York to Philadelphia by way of Powles Hook from thence through Newark and Elizabethtown to Bound Brook and the North Branch of the Raritan to Coryell's Ferry, the only ferry between Newark and Philadelphia noted for its shortness and convenience over the river Delaware." Other announcements were that "Stages would leave the Barley Sheaf Tavern at eight in the morning, arriving at Wells' Ferry twelve hours later. There will be stops for refreshments and changing of horses every ten miles."

The ferry toll house at New Hope now houses the town's public library.

Still other bids for business may be seen in the following announcement: "Stages to leave the Bunch of Grapes at dawn on each Tuesday and the trip will take two days." By 1827 there were three runs each week. The fare was twenty shillings (about five dollars at that time).

Further emphasis on the desirability of travel on the Swift-Sure and other big stage lines could be found in the statement of the former that "Our route over the Old York Road is through the finest, most pleasant and best inhabited part of the state." Apparently, they were selling scenery as well as transportation even in those early days.

At first a trip was made each way once a week by the leading stage companies. Later on, when road conditions were better and more companies began to compete for business, three weekly trips were made. The faster and lighter coaches were more comfortable but they had one disadvantage. They frequently turned over and piled the passengers in a heap.

The Swift-Sure Line was a very profitable operation and it became more so when it was awarded the lucrative mail contracts. Swift-Sure held the contracts until the railroads took them over near the middle of the nineteenth century.

As is the case today with rail and bus lines, the fast through coaches were supplemented by the short-haul lines that operated as feeders to the main lines and for local transportation on the main lines. One of the short-haul lines operated between Flemington and Somerville in 1844 by way of Centerville and Readington. As a growing network of connecting highways developed, the necessary services in connection with the increased road traffic resulted in more villages along the highway.

The huge Conestoga wagon that was used extensively for

freighting on the Old York and other early highways was a very remarkable vehicle. Made in Pennsylvania, originally for carrying hay and other farm products, it later came into general use for overland freighting. Conestogas were designed to meet the primitive conditions under which they had to operate. There were few if any bridges, and road vehicles had to cross streams over fords, sometimes when in flood. The boat-shaped body of the Conestoga was built with flared ends and was so tight it would float in deep water and would keep the passengers and cargo reasonably dry when crossing streams. For really deep water, trees would sometimes be cut and the trunks lashed to the sides of the wagon to add flotation.

To keep out the weather a series of wooden hoops, secured to the sides of the vehicle, formed an arching frame,

A flatboat ferry and cable still in use on the Delaware a few miles north of New Hope.

to which a white canvas top was fastened. Draw ropes were used to pull the front and back together. With the tops on, the rigs stood over twelve feet high. When ready for the road with their four or six horses some of those juggernauts were over sixty feet long.

The wheels of the larger Conestogas were six feet in diameter with wide rims for slogging through the mud. Under the rear axle were the tar bucket and water pail. Loads of up to six tons could be carried. This same type of "covered wagon" was the favorite vehicle used in the wagon-train journeys to California and Oregon during the early and middle part of the nineteenth century.

It must have been a thrilling sight to see the huge wagons and the faster express stages journeying over the Old York Road, up and down the hills of the beautiful countryside of Pennsylvania and through the farmlands of New Jersey. The scene was well described in a poem by David Ely:

> Many a fleet of them
> In one long, upward winding row,
> It was ever a noble sight
> As from the distant mountain height
> Or quiet valley far below,
> Their snow-white covers looked like sails.

There are many amusing descriptions of life as it was during the days of the stages. In *The Story of an Old Farm*, by Andrew D. Mellick, Jr., appears the following:

"Squeezing in on the front seat by the driver's side, our legs and feet were inextricably entangled in mail bags, bundles, whiffletrees and horses' tails. The stage is 'loaded up' three or four to each seat and, with a mountain of luggage piled behind, we rattled down the main street of the town."

There were also plaintive little gems like the following, quoted from Snell's *History of Hunterdon and Somerset Counties:*

> Where is the coach? Where is the mail?
> The coachman, where is he?
> Where is the guard that used to blow
> His horn so cherrily?

Then there was the story of the roustabout who did whatever he could to earn food and drinks. He was known affectionately to the travelers who stopped at the Larison's Corner Tavern as "Gun." The cattlemen, particularly during those days, were a boisterous lot and sometimes not too thoughtful of others. It seemed that "Gun's" star performance to earn a bit of change was to get a running start, butt a wheel of cheese on the bar with his bullet-like head, and shatter it. One day some cattlemen, who had imbibed a bit too much, procured a grindstone and wrapped it in cheesecloth. This was placed on the bar and the unsuspecting roustabout rammed it with his head. After knocking the grindstone to the floor with his head he remarked, "That was the hardest cheese I ever did see."

Many such stories, poems, and legends became a part of the folklore that was built up during the early days of the operation of the Old York Road.

Another one comes from *The Story of American Roads,* by Val Hart:

Oh, it's once I made money by driving a team
But now all is hauled on the railroad by steam,

May the Devil catch the man that's invented the plan
For it's ruined us poor wagoners, and every other man.
Now all you jolly wagoners, who have got good wives,
Go home to your farms and spend your lives.
When your corn is all cribbed and your small grain is
   sowed,
You will have nothing to do but curse the railroad.

For those who may be interested in the folklore of the countryside through which the Old York Road passes, there is a charming little book called *Within a Jersey Circle* by George Quarrie, a visiting Englishman who obtained his material and stories, for the most part, from people living along the road. The book, which was published in 1910, has long been out of print but it may be found in some New Jersey libraries.

It is in this book that we find a vivid description of the actual sight and sound of the arrival of a stage coach. By present-day writing standards it is somewhat redundant but we would like to share it with our readers.

"One of the great personalities of the early stage roads, and in this instance, the Old York Road, was Colonel D. Sanderson. He was the owner and sometimes the driver as well of one of the biggest stage lines between Philadelphia and New York City. In the heyday of his coaching the Colonel's horses were the admiration of every one for their beauty and speed. He had the distinction of selling a pair of bays to the French Emperor for the handsome sum of forty-five hundred dollars. The transaction resulted in all probability through his pleasant and intimate relations with the Marquis de Lafayette who was a frequent traveler over the Old York Road.

"Colonel Sanderson's was a well known and genial face and his figure a commanding one as, seated on his raised 'box' with fares to the right of him, fares to the left of him and more on a second seat behind, he swung into view on the front of his glistening coach. Added to these passengers would generally be six or eight 'insides' and two or three more alongside the conductor, perched high on the 'boot' behind.

"Thus came the great chariot, tearing down the street of the town or village, behind the magnificent, foaming horses, spurred on by a blast of the bugle. The crash of the wheels of the towering equipage, the splendid connecting link between the two great cities of New York and Philadelphia, was inspiring and electrifying to everybody.

"To the passengers, whirled along by those nettled steeds, there was a sympathetic thrill of admiration and a sort of heroic fellowship with the noble animals, in their breasting of terrific steeps and their breakneck thundering down duplicate, rock-bound descents, with all the time, a delectable kaleidoscope of pleasant, pastoral scenes, forests, tumbling floods, sparkling rills and fairy dells. Then there was the exhilarating clatter of hoofs, the rattling, banging and swaying of the laboring vehicle, the merry whistle and the crack of the driver's whip, with his horsey quips and quiddities of stableisms, which the fuming chargers understood perfectly and responded to with the strength of fiery demigods and the docility of children."

No one of this generation is likely to experience anything like the thrill and excitement of waiting for and witnessing the arrival of a horse-drawn stagecoach at a wayside tavern. However, on a quiet summer day in such charming little villages as Reaville or Centerville, it is not hard to imagine

One of the few remaining milestones of the Old York Road. This one, marking twenty-four miles to Philadelphia, has been removed to a nearby farm for safekeeping.

that you can hear the sound of a distant bugle and the beat of the horses' hooves.

In 1764, when the road was completed across the Jerseys from Coryell's Ferry to Elizabethtown Point it resulted in a noticeable improvement of the social contacts between the residents of Pennsylvania and New Jersey. Both New York and Philadelphia showed a marked gain in population which in turn created a greater demand for products carried over the road.

Gentlemen of means sometimes preferred to travel on horseback and, in good weather that means of travel was doubtless more comfortable than bouncing around inside a stage wagon or the later stagecoaches. In the summer, however, it must have been a dusty journey, for not only the fast moving coaches but also light private vehicles stirred up clouds of dust as they whirled along.

Depending upon the condition of the road, the stages seldom arrived at their tavern destinations before sundown. Usually it was much later, particularly the stages on lines like the Swift-Sure that made the run between New York and Philadelphia in thirty hours with only one overnight stop. Whatever the time of arrival, the passengers knew there would be waiting a good hot meal, with a drink or two for those who wanted it. The taverns as a rule served good food even though the overnight accommodations left much to be desired.

Regardless of the time of arrival in the evening, all stages left at daybreak. In the winter, having slept in rooms without heat, the passengers seldom complained. In fact they were glad to get down by the fire in the common room and sit down to the huge breakfast that was the order of the day.

The great volume of travel over the road by private and

The Old York Road passed near the Betsy Ross House in Philadelphia.

stage wagons was a temptation to hold-up men, or road agents, as they were more commonly known. As a result, many men carried pistols to safeguard their valuables. However, the infrequent holdups of the public conveyances on the Old York Road were never as dramatic as those in later years on the western stage lines.

The principal revenue from the operation of the stage lines was of course from passenger traffic. When the mail contracts were secured, almost as soon as the larger lines like the Swift-Sure began operating, the lines were assured of good operating profit. It cost four pence to have a letter carried across the Jerseys.

The charge for carrying freight was a pennyweight for a hundred pounds and such cargo was usually carried in vehicles other than the passenger wagons which were lighter and faster.

During the heyday of stage travel the taverns, inns, or ordinaries as they were variously known, were vital to the operation of the stages and for the accommodation of the general public traveling over the stage roads. The overnight stop on the Swift-Sure line was made at Centerville for a time and later at Flemington, but with the best of luck the travelers on the stages had to endure twelve to fifteen hours of hard travel each day.

Tavern accommodations both for overnight and for meals varied a great deal but those generally to be found on the Old York Road were first class. It is to be assumed that after a day on the road the passengers were not too concerned about the accommodations. From Snell's *History of Hunterdon and Somerset Counties* we learned that, on the fifth of

March 1722, it was "ordered by the court that all publique houses in this county shall pay obedience and deuly observe And keep All the Directions of prices of liquors And other things contained in sd order which shall here After be exprest by the particulars, And that the clerks of the County shall record the same and give a copy to each publique house proprietor in the County. And they shall hang upe the same in some publique place in their severell houses, so that all Travelers And others may have Recourse thereto. And it so shall remain on the penalty of the forfiture of their licenses in case of default—viz., as follows, the prices all to be proclamation money."

Tunison's Tavern in Raritan (later Somerville) was an example of the better inns. With no modesty and, it would appear, somewhat disregarding the truth, this tavern adver-

Within the structure of the present-day Somerset Hotel, it is believed, is part of the original Tunison's Tavern, built in the eighteenth century.

tised, "This is the only tavern between New York and the setting sun." Its published rates set by the court were:

> Lodging four pence; rum by the quartern four pence; brandy do [ditto] six pence; wine by the quart two shillings and eight pence; cider four pence; lunch one shilling two pence; horses stabled and fed one shilling, six pence; oats one half pence per quart.

On the site formerly occupied by Tunison's, at the corner of Main and Grove streets in Somerville, now stands the Somerset Hotel. It is believed that a part of the original tavern is incorporated in the present building. Today, as it was during the height of travel by stage, passengers arrive by coach at the Somerset Hotel but they have had a far more comfortable journey in a modern motor coach.

The typical tavern of the eighteenth century consisted of a large common room with a fireplace. It was here that the landlord had his desk and the room also served as a "tap room" with a recessed space and simple bar from which drinks were dispensed. There were also the diningroom and the kitchen on the first floor. There were several sleeping rooms, depending upon the size of the tavern, on the second floor. Some benches and chairs completed the simple furnishings of the common room. This room was where travelers and local people met in the evenings to gossip and exchange news of the road. In winter a fire was kept burning night and day in the fireplace.

The number of guestrooms varied. Usually several guests had to share a room and when the tavern was crowded, men and women sometimes had to share a room. Late arrivals had to sleep on the floor of the public room or bunk in the barn.

44

In winter the former accommodations were preferred as they shared the blazing fire all night.

The eighteenth-century tavern or inn was, as a rule, the focal point of the community. Town meetings and local business were usually conducted in the public rooms of the taverns. Legal notices of all kinds were posted on the bulletin boards as it was in such locations that the greatest number of people would be sure to see them.

Near every church a tavern could usually be found, and strange as it may seem in this day, the tavern, especially in the winter, was a necessary adjunct to the sometimes all-day services in the unheated churches. The congregation brought their foot warmers, filled with hot coals to provide some degree of comfort. Between the services the men would walk over to the tavern for a warming drink and be braced for another hour or two of worship.

One of the most popular and perhaps the largest tavern on the Old York Road was at Larison's or Pleasant Corners as it was variously known. It was said that "Sporting Corners" would have been a more appropriate name for this place, if all the stories about it may be believed. Frequent dances and other social affairs in the tavern attracted young people from as far away as Easton. In the winter they came on sleighing parties and on coaching parties in the summer. On those festive occasions the entire lower floor of the tavern would be converted into a ballroom by folding back the partitions, converting the several first-floor rooms into one area for dancing. The local tavern usually was the only building in the community large enough to accommodate such gatherings and, as the stage travelers were usually invited to participate, it made for a very gay evening after a day on the road. These events gave the tavern some social prestige.

A friend of ours told us that her mother used to drive in a buggy with her escort all the way from Flemington to Princeton, and dance until the small hours of the morning. The couple would then start the drive home, a distance of twenty-five miles, stopping for breakfast at Larison's Tavern near dawn. Today on our good roads such a drive would be a matter of forty minutes each way.

Larison's Tavern was rumored to have a somewhat sinister side. There was a small room on the second floor, without windows and with but a single small door. Poorly lighted by candles, it was a room of scary shadows. It was in that little room that the professional gamblers played cards with the cattle drovers and the more sportive local men. The "locals" and the drovers never won, of course, and never seemed to get any wiser. The room was heated in the winter by a Franklin stove and the nightly scene was described by one early writer: "The shadows cast by the candles on the tense faces of the card players created an aura of evil over the whole scene." It is said that large sums were won and lost in a single night's session and the games continued until dawn. The professionals would move on to another tavern to fleece a new crop of suckers the next night. When we stop to think about current investigations and probes into crime, times haven't changed very much.

Around most of the wayside inns and taverns there were acres of meadow for the herds of cattle or flocks of sheep the drovers were taking to market. Some of the cattle were driven to local markets from as far away as Ohio. In the summer a cloud of dust on a highway usually indicated a band of sheep being driven to market. This meant good business for the taverns and the drovers were welcomed, particularly in the bars, but the tavern owners very prudently posted signs in the rooms reading, "Cattle drovers must remove their boots before getting into bed." The cattle were bedded down in the tavern meadows, and sometimes were auctioned from the verandah of the tavern.

While many of the early stage taverns are still standing and, in fact, many of them are still serving the public as they have been doing for over a century or two, the famous Larison's is no more. It slowly disintegrated into a complete ruin and, as is so often the case with our historic places, it has been replaced with a gas station.

Edward Field in his book, *The Colonial Taverns*, writes of the intimate relations of the taverns, inns, and the old churches and the curious interdependency, one on the other, as local institutions. The roadside hostelries were known as taverns in New Jersey and New York. In Pennsylvania the designation of "inn" was more common. In the South it was usually an "ordinary."

Inns and taverns at times played an important part in the affairs of our country. Thomas Jefferson wrote the Declaration of Independence in the Indian Queen Tavern in Philadelphia, where he was staying at the time. Many stirring meetings of the Committees of Safety were held in local taverns and inns throughout the Colonies, before the Revolution started. The landlords as a rule were sympathetic to the American cause.

At Bound Brook, on the Old York Road, formerly stood the Middlebrook Hotel, first known as Harris' Tavern, when it was built about 1700. The tavern was known for years as one of the finest and most popular on the stage road. It was located near the Middlebrook which was and still is the western boundary of the town of Bound Brook and it was halfway between New Brunswick and Somerville. The early

Dutch settlers, driving up the Raritan Valley to seek land beyond "The Forks," favored the tavern, as did the travelers on the stage road.

When the railroad was built near the middle of the nineteenth century, it left the tavern in a corner across the tracks and a new turnpike added to its isolation. Ike Bennett, a veteran stage driver, refused to change his route and for many years continued to cross the tracks with his stage and dine at the tavern. One day his stage was hit by a train, and although he and his horses escaped injury, he drove no more. Ike never forgave the railroad for ruining the stage business and the accident ended the business of the stage line in that part of the Raritan Valley.

The Harris or Fisher Tavern was also noted for the fact that the first Masonic Lodge in Somerset County was reputedly organized there. During the Revolution it is known that Masonic meetings were held in this building from time to time. The tavern was said to have been the favorite rendezvous of the men and officers of both armies. Perhaps that is why it survived the war.

Some historians have questioned whether Harris' Tavern survived the raids and burning by the British during the Revolution. The building was still standing after the beginning of the twentieth century, and what was left of it was razed about 1917. Rings in the smoke-grimed ceiling from the British musket barrels could clearly be seen. The authors can assure the reader that this is a fact as we saw the marks many times.

Among the most colorful symbols of the early inns and taverns were the wooden pictorial signs that usually hung over the entrance of the buildings. During the early years of

The sign of the Crossed Keys Hotel. (*Courtesy of the Mercer Museum, Doylestown.*)

the Colonies such signs were used by not only the taverns but other businesses as well. The pictures, painted on the signs— a boot, cleaver, fish, or similar symbols indicating the character of the business—served two purposes. One was for the benefit of those who could not read; the other was simply the desire for an attractive sign. For example, the sign might show a picture of a sheaf of wheat, and name, "The Wheat Sheaf Tavern." The "Gen'l Greene" sign had a portrait of that Revolutionary hero. Equally attractive signs hung in front of the Indian Queen, Logan's Inn, and many other taverns along the old roads. Some were truly works of primitive art. On occasion the innkeeper exhibited a sense of humor, as in the case of a tavern of somewhat unsavory character, whose sign had a beehive painted on it and underneath was lettered:

> Here in this hive we're all alive
> Good liquor makes us funny,
> If you are dry, stop in and try
> The flavor of our honey.

It is difficult to find those old wooden tavern or store signs today. Once in a while one does turn up in some antique shop but, like the one-time plentiful wooden Indians, it quickly disappears into a private collection or a museum. One of the largest and finest collections in the area is in the Mercer Museum in Doylestown, Pennsylvania. That museum, built in 1916 by Dr. Henry Chapman Mercer, contains what is believed to be the largest collection of implements, tools, artifacts, etc., with which the early Americans lived. These are well worth seeing for those interested in such things. When driving over the Old York Road from New Hope or Philadelphia it is only a few miles from Buckingham to

Doylestown and it is open every day in the week and on Sunday in the summer.

Though most stage travelers on the Old York Road preferred to end their land journey at the Elizabethtown Point Ferry, some continued on to Newark and over the Newark to Bergen road and the Paterson Plank Road to the Powles Hook (Jersey City) Ferry. From the ferry it was just a short trip across the Hudson to Manhattan.

On the journey across the meadows, passengers were frequently delayed because of the swampy conditions in places on the road. At times the stage would get bogged down to the axles. These conditions were improved some in places as on the Paterson Plank Road where split cedar logs were laid to form a corduroy road.

The vast area of the meadows, some thirty thousand acres in extent, was a natural barrier to travel between the Hudson and the Newark-Hackensack area for many years. In fact, on C. C. Vermule's official map, drawn in 1887, only one road was shown crossing the meadows. That was the Paterson Plank Road. On that same map Vermule indicates quite a number of cedar forest areas, one of which was the Secaucus Upland and Bog through which part of the stage road passed. It was from those forests that the cedar logs were cut to make the corduroy roads.

In 1764 a new road was built between Newark and Bergen, which connected with the Paterson Plank Road and thus continued to the ferry. Another and earlier road had extended from the ferry to Staten Island and by still another ferry to Elizabethtown Point. The Swift-Sure Stage Line used this route for a time until the shorter and faster Newark-Bergen road was built.

There has been considerable discussion among writers and historians as to whether the meadows are on the site of a prehistoric glacier lake; and whether, when the glacier receded, the land rose over the present area and left dry land which supported a wide variety of plant life, including many stands of white cedar. During our efforts to resolve this question we were not certain whether or not it was all a legend. However, through the help of a friend in the State Highway Department we were given a copy of a paper entitled "History of An Esturine Bog at Secaucus, N.J." From the careful research done by C. J. Heusser, its author, we are convinced that Lake Hackensack did in fact exist and that the land did rise and that it supported freshwater flora including cedar forests. In fact a dozen or so stark cedar tree trunks, blackened by fire, may be seen today from the Turnpike as it nears Route 46.

Many factors contributed to the final disappearance of the cedar trees and the meadows are now infiltrated with salt water, and nothing but salt grasses grow there. For many years, in fact, well into the present century, the salt hay was harvested and used for packing material in the shipping of fragile articles. It was also used to separate layers of natural ice when it was harvested and stored in the ice houses of the day.

With the successful application of the newly-invented steam engine to boats and later to rail locomotives, the end of profitable stage operation was in sight. The former sail ferries could no longer successfully compete with the new faster steam ferries.

The first steam ferry was named the *Raritan* and it was

owned by John and Robert Livingston, the backers of Robert Fulton in the development of the *Clermont*. Colonel Ogden, a member of one of the first families to settle in what is now Elizabeth, put his steam ferry *Atlanta* in service soon thereafter.

Considerable rivalry existed between the steamboat owners, and it is related that the competition was so keen that some of the captains of the ferries would stand on the dock and call to prospective passengers, "Right this way! Free passage to New York City, including a good dinner." It has a familiar ring. Remember the gasoline wars of our day? Soon the new steamboats were not only operating a ferry service between New York and Elizabeth; they also ran lines directly between New York and New Brunswick. Like all competitions, this new way of travel straightened itself out and those who had survived found it a very profitable business. The Vanderbilts and other business tycoons moved in on it and many fortunes were founded on the early steamboat business.

Some of the ferry lines, in an effort to take business away from the stages, made connections with the entrance of the Delaware and Raritan Canal, which opened in 1834, and thus travelers could continue in a leisurely way by canal packet to Bordentown on the Delaware. As a way of travel it was cleaner and more comfortable than the stages, but it was too slow to compete with the railroads that began operating soon after the opening of the canal.

With the opening of the railroad from Elizabethport to Plainfield in 1839, and on to Somerville in 1849, travelers began to transfer to the nearest rail point and thus the through stage traffic was lost, mile by mile. Railroads also

Stagecoaches of the Raritan & Somerville Line that ran until 1898.
(*Courtesy of the Somerset* Messenger Gazette.)

took over the mail contracts, and this spelled the end of the colorful era of stage travel.

The short-haul lines continued for a few years, serving passengers for journeys between towns and from places where rail service was not yet available. One of the last of the stage lines on the Old York Road was that operated by Henry and John Frech between Somerville and Raritan until 1898. The extension of the electric trolley line from New Brunswick to Raritan ended the days of that stage line.

It seems so long ago that stages began operating on our famous road, and yet it is only a matter of a bit over two hundred years which isn't really long in the history of a country. The stage lines rendered a valuable service and helped to improve the economic conditions in the Colonies. Next came the canals and the railroads and then the electric trolley lines. Each brought better and faster transportation, each in turn eventually putting the earlier method out of business. Now the airlines are getting the passenger business with two-thousand-mile an hour supersonic jets just ahead. In some states passenger trains no longer run. Who knows what will come next?

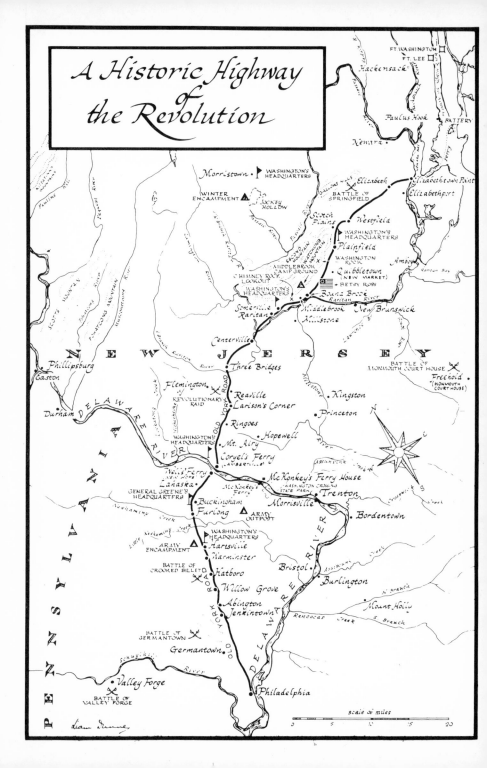

# II

# The Old York Road in the Revolution

"Washington Crossing the Delaware," a painting by Emanuel Leutze, depicts the famous Christmas night crossing by Washington and twelve hundred men. The picture was purchased from the artist in 1897 by John S. Kennedy and presented to the Metropolitan Museum of Art, and is now on permanent loan to the Pennsylvania State Park at Washington's Crossing. (*Reproduced by permission of the Metropolitan Museum of Art.*)

AND HERE
IN THIS PLACE OF SACRIFICE
IN THIS VALE OF HUMILIATION
IN THIS VALLEY OF THE SHADOW
OF THAT DEATH OUT OF WHICH
THE LIFE OF AMERICA ROSE
REGENERATE AND FREE
LET US BELIEVE
WITH AN ABIDING FAITH
THAT TO THEM
UNION WILL SEEM AS DEAR
AND LIBERTY AS SWEET
AND PROGRESS AS GLORIOUS
AS THEY WERE TO OUR FATHERS
AND ARE TO YOU AND ME
AND THAT THE INSTITUTIONS
WHICH HAVE MADE US HAPPY
PRESERVED BY THE
VIRTUE OF OUR CHILDREN
SHALL BLESS
THE REMOTEST GENERATION
OF THE TIME TO COME

HENRY ARMITT BROWN

From the inscription on the Memorial Arch at Valley Forge.

The Old York Road from Philadelphia to Elizabethtown
Point had been in full operation as a stage road for more
than ten years when the War for Independence began in
1776. Just as civilian travelers had preferred this road as
the fastest and most direct route between Philadelphia and
New York, the Continental military forces early recognized
its strategic and tactical value in the coming struggle.

In the years before the war, feeder roads with their short-
haul stage lines and freight-carrying vehicles had increased
the commercial traffic across the middle of New Jersey. During the first few months of the war, first the through stage
lines ceased to operate, and one by one the short-haul lines
also discontinued for the duration. Thereafter, until the war
was over, the Old York Road was used almost entirely for
the movement of troops and supplies, and by the couriers
who kept the lines of communication open. This road, together with the natural fortress of the Watchung Hills,
formed the basis on which Washington's plan to hold the
Jerseys depended.

In the late summer of 1776, following the defeat of the
American Army on Long Island, the Westchester reverses,
and the abandonment of Fort Washington and Fort Lee,
Washington withdrew his forces to the Hackensack Valley.
When it was learned that the British were moving over the
river with the apparent intention of engaging the Conti-

The Van Horn House at Bound Brook, now a clubhouse for employees of American Cyanamid Company.

nentals somewhere in North Jersey, Washington realized that his position between the Hackensack and Passaic Rivers might well prove to be a trap the British could easily spring. Following a council of war, it was decided that the American forces should be withdrawn from the valley. Washington directed the evacuation to and across the Acquackanonk Bridge and then on to Newark. Heavy rains made the movement of guns and supplies almost impossible. When the Continentals moved out of Newark and over the Old York Road to New Brunswick, the British were not far behind. However, Washington crossed the Raritan at New Brunswick far enough in advance of the British forces to destroy the bridge. For some reason not clear, the American Army stayed on the west shore of the Raritan and withstood a heavy artillery attack from the British. Later on, the retreat was resumed over the "Old Dutch Road" (now Route 27) toward Princeton. Leaving a rear guard of about twelve hundred men under General William Alexander, known as Lord Stirling, and General Adam Stephen, Washington and the balance of his force continued to Trenton. Having successfully reached the shore of the Delaware, where all the boats on the river had been assembled, Washington returned to Princeton to await events. The British soon crossed the Raritan in pursuit of the Continentals and continued their march toward Kingston and Princeton. Washington, Stirling, and Stephen, who together with twelve hundred men had been left at Princeton as a rear guard to protect the main army proceeding to Trenton, slowly withdrew to Trenton with the British in close pursuit. With his entire command on the Jersey shore of the Delaware River with all available boats awaiting the arrival of their Commander-in-Chief, the American forces crossed the river to the Pennsylvania side. It is said that the British arrived at Trenton as the last of the American Army was in midstream.

When the British learned that there was not a single boat left on the Jersey shore they withdrew to New Brunswick for the winter. They posted small forces at Mount Holly and Burlington, and a larger force of Hessians at Trenton. Many of the officers of the British army continued on to New York and more comfortable winter quarters.

Washington posted his forces along the Pennsylvania side of the Delaware River from Bristol to Wells' Ferry. The time was an unusually cold December and the troops had little or no shelter. To make it worse, many were ill. Few were adequately clothed and there was not enough food for

The Wallace House in Somerville, Washington's headquarters during the encampment at Middlebrook.

the men who had endured so much suffering—reverses in battle, long marches across the Jerseys, and an encampment in the bitter cold.

One bright note in the gloomy picture was the welcome addition to the army of two thousand Pennsylvania militia.

A stalemate now existed. The morale of the soldiers, and in fact of the people of the Colonies, was at its lowest ebb. The British were in possession of the Jerseys and General Washington knew that despite the condition of his army and the seeming impossibility of retaking New Jersey, he had to plan some dramatic stroke soon or admit defeat.

A council of war was called at the Thompson-Neely House, just a few miles below the Old York Road at Wells' Ferry. General Nathanael Greene, who had made Bogart's Inn his headquarters, rode north over the Old York Road to join the council. As soon as the officers were assembled, discussions were begun and they lasted for several days and nights.

In the meantime, Washington ordered Captain Daniel Bray to gather up remaining boats on the river as far north as Easton as a further protection against a surprise foray by the British patrols. The boats were hidden behind Malta Island, below Wells' Ferry. Thirty-five boats were secured and half of them were the forty-four- and sixty-six-foot Durham boats, in which horses and cannon could be safely transported.

Many plans were discussed at the council and finally General Washington suggested a stroke so bold that it seemed

The Staats House at South Bound Brook, later known as the La Tourette House. The center section was built prior to 1690. The house was headquarters for General Frederick von Steuben, Washington's inspector general, during the Middlebrook encampment.

impossible of success. Washington's plan was to make a surprise attack on the British at Trenton, following a crossing of the ice-filled river at McKonkey's Ferry on Christmas night.

Preparations were begun immediately, and the crossing and subsequent victory at Trenton wrote a glorious chapter in American history.

To understand something of what Washington and his men endured during that bitter December in 1776 we suggest that the reader drive along the river road on some cold winter afternoon. Stand for a few moments at the actual point of embarkation and you will experience an emotional sense of history no mere reading about the event will give.

Every day, at half-hour intervals, a stirring narration about the "crossing" may be heard in the memorial building auditorium in Pennsylvania Washington Crossing Park. It will be an experience long remembered.

The magnificent painting, "Washington Crossing the Delaware," which hung for many years in the Metropolitan Museum of Art, is now permanently installed in the Memorial Auditorium in the Park. There are those who object to this painting, pointing out that it is not an authentic representation of the crossing; that the thirteen-star flag had not been designed at the time; that Washington's position in the prow of a rowboat is an impossible one; and that the ice-covered river is the Rhine, not the Delaware. All of this seems immaterial to the authors.

The picture is the most famous one of a series of paintings on American historical themes, done by a German-born American artist, Emanuel Leutze, in his studio at Dusseldorf around the middle of the nineteenth century. Leutze had spent an entire summer at Taylorsville absorbing the historic atmosphere of the area and he consulted with historians and official sources. This is not intended to be a photograph, but a dramatic conception of the most daring exploit of the Revolutionary War; it has become one of our national treasures, a cherished symbol of American heroism.

Near the Thompson-Neely House, a short way below the Old York Road at New Hope, which was Wells' Ferry during the Revolution, are the graves of many of the soldiers who died of disease or exposure during the encampment there.

Historians disagree as to whether the first battle at Trenton and the victory at Princeton soon after were the turning point in the war. It was certainly the turning point in the morale of the troops and of the patriots in the Colonies.

On the bank of the Delaware River in Pennsylvania's Washington Crossing Park lie the men of the Continental army who died in camp during December, 1776.

"House of Decision," the Thompson-Neely House in Washington Crossing State Park, Pennsylvania.

The man who should be the best judge in the matter is Lord Cornwallis himself. He expressed it this way at a victory dinner given by General Washington after the surrender at Yorktown: In a toast to General Washington Lord Cornwallis said, "Your Excellency, may I sincerely congratulate you on your splendid victory and may I say that I believe that when the illustrious part which your Excellency has borne in the long and arduous contest becomes a matter of history, fame will gather your brightest laurels from the banks of the Delaware rather than those of the Chesapeake."

Following the miserable winter at Morristown and Jockey Hollow, where the suffering of the soldiers was almost beyond human endurance, with snow at times over four feet in depth, Washington ordered the army to move down to the First Watchung Mountain. He had, during his winter planning, devised a new strategy, realizing as he did the impossibility of meeting the well-trained British in the open field. The loss of five thousand men at the battle of Long Island had proved this. Therefore, Washington decided to utilize the natural fortress of the Watchung Hills that extended across North Jersey. With few passes to be guarded and the Old York Road below, close by in the valley for the quick movement of troops and supplies to the east or west as the occasion demanded, the whole situation was ideal as a summer base camp from which forays against the British could be carried out. In addition, a nearby lookout, a rock formation extending out from the mountain, made possible a close watch of the British at New Brunswick and, in fact, on a clear day Howe's fleet in New York Harbor could be seen.

In May, 1777, the orders were issued to move out and the army moved down to the south face of the First Watchung Mountain, north of Bound Brook. Camp was established and earthworks were thrown up below to insure the army against surprise attack from directly below or from the east or west over the Old York Road. Back of the First Mountain near present-day Martinsville, two earth redoubts were constructed and a patrol left in each to guard against a flanking movement. With the passes well guarded, Washington had established an impregnable position.

In the meantime, the British were still in position at New Brunswick and beginning to send out patrols trying to induce Washington's army to come down out of their mountain stronghold and "fight like men." Washington did not accept

The Continental Army's Watchung lookout, now known as
Washington Rock.

the invitation and knew that he could continue to control the situation so that when an opportunity offered, his men could move to a favorable position to fight on his own terms. The value of the Old York Road in the situation cannot be over-emphasized, for fast movement of troops and supplies and as an easy route for the couriers who were constantly on the road.

At Camp Middlebrook there were only eight thousand men, of whom a thousand were unfit for service as a result of their suffering in camp the previous winter.

Having established his forces in the two strong positions at Camp Middlebrook and at the pass at Chimney Rock, Washington kept a lookout at what is now called Washington Rock to observe any movement of the British army or of the fleet in New York Harbor.

Apparently Washington lacked any positive information about the intentions of either the British army or of the fleet. At one point it appeared that the British were leaving New Jersey as they were seen moving to Perth Amboy and being ferried over to Staten Island. During the movement to Perth Amboy the British had to fight a rear-guard action against Morgan's Raiders, who harassed them during the whole march. By June 30, 1777, all enemy forces were out of New Jersey and it was again in possession of the Continentals.

Washington was still uncertain whether Howe was going to sail his fleet up the Hudson or south to Philadelphia. To be in a position to counter any move, Washington ordered his forces to move over the Old York Road toward Pompton Plains. If the British plan was to sail up the Hudson and cut New England from the southern colonies, Washington

69

Camp Middlebrook at Bound Brook, where the thirteen-star flag flies twenty-four hours a day.

wanted to be near enough to the upper Hudson to prevent such a move.

The fleet was seen to move out, not up the Hudson, but toward the south. Washington ordered his troops back onto the Old York Road for a fast march across New Jersey to the Delaware River. He still was uncertain as to whether the British would sail up the Delaware to Trenton and attempt to take possession of the Delaware Valley or whether they would be content to take Philadelphia.

Having arrived at Coryell's Ferry, Washington sent Lord Stirling across the river to set up his battery and earthworks to resist the British if they made an overland attack from Philadelphia, over the Old York Road or up by way of the Pennsylvania shore.

Washington was quartered in the home of Richard Holcombe, General Greene at the home of George Coryell, and

The Holcombe House at Lambertville, Washington's headquarters in 1777. Lafayette was also a guest there.

Generals Hamilton, Stephen, and Lincoln at other nearby homes.

The many errors of judgment on the part of the British commanders have been dealt with extensively by historians, but no one seems to have realized that by overlooking the value of taking possession of the Old York Road and preventing its use by the Continental Army, an opportunity to confine Washington to his mountain fortress was lost.

It has been argued that the British could not have taken possession of the Old York Road at any point because the militia and the patriots of the countryside would have prevented it. Possibly this is so, but we believe the British did not realize at any time during the struggle how essential the road was to Washington and that they therefore lost a good chance to pin down the Continental army. It is also likely that the road could have been taken without too much resistance because so many people of the area were ardent Tories and would have doubtless helped in the attempt to take the road. At least it's an interesting speculation on the possibilities, had it been taken and held by the British for the duration of the war.

While waiting at Coryell's Ferry, Washington wrote to Congress, then in session in Philadelphia: "Having received word regarding Howe's intention to take Philadelphia, the main body of the army will begin its march down the Old York Road toward that city."

Fearing capture, Congress fled to York, Pennsylvania. Thereupon, Washington moved his troops down to Germantown, five miles from Philadelphia, to be near enough to defend Philadelphia if Howe's fleet sailed up the Delaware.

Receiving no further information as to the whereabouts

72

The Moland House at Hartsville, Washington's headquarters in August 1777.

of the British fleet, Washington withdrew his forces back up the Old York Road to the Neshaminy Hills, near the Cross Roads. He made his headquarters in the Moland House and the army camped along the road.

The Continental army at this point were not the raw, untrained troops of a year earlier. The majority were seasoned veterans. Even the militia units were trained and hardened in combat and could give a good account of themselves in battle, as it became apparent at the battle of the Brandywine and at Germantown.

For nearly two weeks Washington stayed at his headquarters at the Cross Roads, waiting for information as to the whereabouts of the British fleet. Word was finally received that the fleet had been sighted off the Maryland coast in Chesapeake Bay. He then issued the following order:

GENERAL ORDERS

The Cross Roads Headquarters
August 21, 1777

The whole army is to march tomorrow morning, the General to beat at half past three; the Troop at half past four and at five o'clock the troops begin their march. The Major Generals, Quarter Master General and the Commissary General will receive their orders at Headquarters at five o'clock this afternoon. An orderly man from each regiment of horse to attend at that time for orders.

George Washington
*Commander-in-Chief*

With the army on the march down the Old York Road to Philadelphia was the young Frenchman, the Marquis de Lafayette, who had been sworn in as a major general at the Moland House headquarters the day before by General Washington.

Washington had two objectives in mind for the march to Philadelphia. One was to quiet the fears of the populace, who had heard that the British were on their way to take the city. Washington believed that by parading his entire army through the city he could stiffen the morale of the people. His other thought was to plan to meet the British outside the city and to defend it against invasion. When it was learned that Howe apparently was going to land his troops at the head of Chesapeake Bay, instead of at some point such as Chester on the Delaware, Washington decided to precipitate the battle at a point of his own choice. The place he

The Drake House in Plainfield, used by Washington as a meeting place with his spies and scouts, has been restored by local organizations and is now a museum.

selected was Chadd's Ford on Brandywine Creek. The result of that encounter could be considered a draw as Washington, despite his immediate loss, was able to withdraw to the safety of the Schuylkill hills.

At the beginning of October, Washington decided to try again to draw the British out of Philadelphia, which they had occupied following their victory at Brandywine. Four lines of troops were moved down the Bethlehem Pike and the Old York Road toward Germantown. Washington hoped to encircle the British when they came out of Philadelphia to meet him.

Germantown turned out to be another Brandywine, for on October 4, 1777, the tide of battle turned against the

75

Continentals and, despite the valiant account they had given of their ability to fight, the American forces had to break off the engagement and move out. Again the Old York Road enabled the army to withdraw successfully some of the command east over the roads about twenty miles before they made camp near Pennypacker's Mill. The nearness of the Old York Road to Valley Forge was an important factor when the army went into camp that winter.

While the army was suffering from lack of food and clothing and stricken with disease during that terrible winter at Valley Forge another condition added to their misery. It was the great number of Tories along the Old York Road, particularly those who sold their farm products to the British in Philadelphia instead of to the starving Americans. There were not enough men in good health to man patrols to stop the practice.

In the middle of the winter, or so it seemed, Washington wrote the following letter to Congress. It was dated December 23, 1777.

I am now convinced without a doubt, that unless some great change suddenly takes place . . . this army must inevitably be reduced to one or other of these three things. Starve, dissolve or disperse, in order to obtain subsistence in the best manner they can: rest assured Sirs this is not an exaggerated picture, but that I have abundant reason to support what I say.

British foraging parties constantly raided farms along the Old York Road and those patriots who held out farm products for the American forces were treated harshly by the raiding British. Less and less food was available for the starving troops at Valley Forge.

76

Cattle were driven over the Old York Road from other areas and, when they could get them through to the camp at Valley Forge, the troops could have meat. One cattle drover, with a good-sized herd of cattle, asked General Lacey for a military escort as he neared Hatboro. The drover feared the British raiding parties would capture the desperately needed cattle. Lacey refused because he could not spare any of his command for escort duty. As a result, when the drover with his precious cattle had left the Old York Road and were only a few miles from the camp, the cattle were confiscated by a British raiding party.

Both British and the American patrols constantly searched the countryside for supplies, but food of all kinds was scarce. Lacey did his best with his small command to stop the smuggling of food into Philadelphia. All roads leading into Philadelphia were patrolled, particularly the Old York Road over which most of the supplies were going. On several occasions Lacey and his small force barely escaped capture, when they operated too close to the British lines.

Thomas Paine well reflected the feeling of the desperate men at Valley Forge when he wrote: "These are the times that try men's souls; the summer soldier and the sunshine patriot will, in this crisis, shrink from the service of their country; but he that stands it now deserves the love and thanks of men and women. Tyranny, like hell, is not easily conquered.

"Yet we have this consolation with us, that the harder the conflict, the more glorious the triumph."

Some historians contend that the suffering at Valley Forge, during the winter of 1777-78, was due largely to the inefficient management of the Commissary General Joseph Trumbull of Connecticut. A more important factor was that

Graves of Revolutionary soldiers in the churchyard of Old First Church in Elizabeth.

both the British in Philadelphia and the American forces at Valley Forge were trying to live that winter off of a small area of countryside that had been stripped almost bare of food.

General Lacey and his patrol were trying to seal off Hatboro, where the Tories were still successfully getting food to the British, and one night the General and his four hundred men were in camp near the Crooked Billet Tavern. Early in the morning of May 1, 1778, a large British patrol that had been tipped off as to Lacey's whereabouts surprised the American force, and before that skirmish, as it is known in history, was over, it had cost Lacey twenty-six men killed and twenty-eight wounded and missing. Fighting a rear-guard action,

78

Lacey was able to save his command and they retired up the Old York Road. As a result the British held the Old York Road as far east as the Cross Roads, near the Neshaminy.

When word of the disastrous engagement reached Washington at Valley Forge he again wrote to Congress at York. "Every kind of villainy is carried on by the people near the enemy lines and, from their general conduct, I am induced to believe that but few real friends to America are left within ten miles of Philadelphia."

With the coming of spring, conditions were somewhat better at the Valley Forge encampment. Lacey had gained possession again of the Old York Road to a point below Hatboro and, in response to Washington's desperate pleas, cattle were moved in from western Pennsylvania and the Jersey

Replicas of the log huts in which Continental soldiers lived during the winter at Valley Forge.

The General Greene Inn at Buckingham Crossing, originally Bogart's Tavern. The first Bucks County Committee for Safety met here, and it was General Greene's headquarters in 1776.

provinces. For the first time there was enough food for the troops.

When word was received in the spring of 1778 of the intention of the British to evacuate Philadelphia, Washington decided to follow on a route over the Old York Road to Wells' Ferry that would put his forces close enough to engage the British. The British moved out in mid-June, over the road to Bristol and across the Delaware River at that point, with the apparent intention of crossing the Jerseys.

On June 19th, Washington ordered General Charles Lee and his six brigades to march to Wells' Ferry. Lafayette and Baron de Kalb were to follow the next day with Washington and the balance of the troops. All the forces of weather hampered that march. Rain had so mired the Old York Road that it was almost impossible to move the guns over it. The General was forced to stop overnight at Buckingham. He arrived at Coryell's Ferry on June 21st. Lee and his men had crossed the Delaware at that point the night before and were proceeding toward Hopewell in Jersey, having dragged their guns by main strength up over Goat Hill Road from Coryell's Ferry. Even today, with the modern road that surmounts that hill, the grades are terrific. One can well visualize what an almost superhuman task it must have been to get horses and guns over the road as it was during that stormy night in June, 1778.

Daniel Morgan and his raiders were ordered down the Delaware Valley to locate the British and harass their rear.

The events of the meeting of the two armies near Mon-

Friends' Meetinghouse at Lahaska, built in 1768, and used as a military hospital during the Revolution.

General John Lacey and his patrol of four hundred men were ambushed here and severely mauled in a night-time battle.

mouth Court House are too well known to repeat here. However, it was once again the Old York Road that made possible the quick march of the Army from Valley Forge to the battlefield. While the battle was not a clear-cut victory for the Continentals, it did again boost the morale of the troops.

As the final days of the epic struggle for independence made the American people more confident of eventual success, the now hardened and confident army moved south to Virginia. The surrender of the British at Yorktown was the final act in the long struggle for freedom for which the men of the Continental army and the militia of the various Colonies had fought so long and so hard.

On a tablet in the memorial tower at Bowman's Hill in Washington Crossing Park is inscribed a short tribute that aptly sums up the feeling of the American people following the victory and surrender at Yorktown:

It may be doubted whether so small a number of men ever employed so short a space of time with greater or more lasting results upon the history of the world.

Does it sound familiar? We wonder if it could have possibly inspired the famous statement of Winston Churchill during World War II when he said, "Never in the field of human conflict was so much owed by so many to so few."

"General Washington," "Benjamin Franklin," and attendants at the Nassau Tavern in Princeton during the re-enactment in 1939 of Washington's coach journey to New York for his inauguration.

# III

# The Old York Road Today

The Old York Road at Centerville. Here in this pre-Revolutionary village are many reminders of the days when the local tavern was the overnight stop for the Swift-Sure stagecoaches.

The authors, having enjoyed so many interesting days exploring the Old York Road, hope that their readers will also want to see the many historic places on this highway of the past. For those who enjoy, as we do, spending a summer day wandering along an old road, stopping here and there to savor the charm of things and places of an earlier day, a personally guided tour over the Old York Road would be in order. So come along and let us tell you about it. On an exploring trip like this, one should not hurry. Perhaps several days should be devoted to it.

Our highway can be explored with the starting point at either end, whichever is most convenient. Doubtless the people of New Jersey will want to start their exploration at Elizabeth and continue over the entire road to Front and Arch Streets in Philadelphia. Others may prefer to reverse the route. On our journey together through the pages of this book we shall start at Elizabeth as it is known today, or Elizabethtown, as it was called in the seventeenth century.

Today the eastern end of the road is an unattractive industrial area on Newark Bay with nothing left of the original ferry. The actual site of the ferry is marked by the rotting piles of a later dock. It was here, at the end of present-day Elizabeth Avenue in Elizabethport, that the early sail ferries departed for Manhattan as far back as 1679. Here also, General Washington and his wife stepped down from their coach

87

The Old First Church in Elizabeth.

on their journey from Mount Vernon to New York in 1789. At the ferry they boarded a gaily decorated barge which carried them to the Battery in Manhattan for Washington's inauguration as the first President of the United States.

Present-day Elizabeth is a city with a great historic heritage and Old First Church and the churchyard beside it are indeed hallowed ground. It was in the original building that the General Assembly met from 1666 to 1682. The present building was erected in 1789 and, except for the lack of the former tall steeple, it remains today about as it was nearly two centuries ago. The city also bears the distinction of being the oldest English-speaking community in New Jersey and Old First Church was the first in which services were conducted in English. During the Colonial and early Federal periods Elizabeth had a large and active group of the Sons of Liberty and other patriotic organizations and many descendants of the members still observe and cherish the distinctive past of their city.

Boxwood Hall, on East Jersey Street, was the home of Elias Boudinot, the first President of the Continental Congress. Later, he introduced the resolution in the U.S. House of Representatives that caused President Washington to proclaim November 26, 1789, our first Thanksgiving Day. After the murder of Parson Caldwell at Elizabethtown Point his body was thrown on the steps of Boudinot Hall. The British intended it as a warning to the American patriots, but after hearing the fiery speech delivered by Boudinot, while standing over the Parson's body, the Patriots were more determined than ever to get rid of British rule.

Just beyond the northern boundary of the city still stands Liberty Hall which was built in 1773 by William Livingston, the first Governor of the State of New Jersey. It was in this

Boxwood Hall in Elizabeth.

house that Sally, the Governor's daughter, married John Jay, who later became the First Chief Justice of the United States. The Washingtons, Alexander Hamilton, the Marquis de Lafayette and many other illustrious people of the Colonial period were frequent guests here.

Where the Public Library now stands, on the corner of Broad Street and Rahway Avenue, the latter the Old York Road, formerly stood several famous stage taverns. Among them were the Indian Queen and Cornelisse's.

Much of the original route of our road from Elizabeth to Westfield is lost today in a maze of streets and highways. Therefore the next point of interest on our journey will be Westfield's historic Presbyterian Church. The first log church, which stood near the site of the present building, was erected in 1735. The present church was built in 1861. The bell from an earlier church that was rung to warn the Patriots of the approach of the British hangs in the belfry of the present building. The earlier church was the scene of the trial and conviction of James Morgan, a British soldier who was hanged at "Gallows Hill" on North Broad Street. It was Morgan who murdered "Fighting Parson" Caldwell in Elizabethtown.

In 1684 some Scottish immigrants, who had landed at Perth Amboy, followed an Indian path north toward the Watchung hills, looking for a place to settle. They found a location to their liking and so they decided to make that area their home. The only possessions they could bring with them were the tools, seeds, and other things that could be carried on their backs. Thus the present-day Scotch Plains came into being.

The path those settlers used to travel north was bisected at the settlement by an east-west Indian path at the place where the immigrants settled. This path later became a part of the Old York Road.

The old tavern that is still standing on Front Street served travelers on the Old York Road for a century or more. The center part of the present building dates back to 1737. This venerable building has been continuously occupied, either as an inn or as a residence, since it was built. Surrounding the tavern today are several shops of Colonial design that add to the charm of the place.

Continuing our journey west on Front Street to and through Plainfield, we are still following approximately the original stage route. Depending upon the old map or text source consulted, there seem to be some divergent opinions about the course of the road from Plainfield west to Bound Brook. Old maps show the road going to New Market after leaving Plainfield, and we believe much of the confusion is due to the fact that New Market, or Quibbletown, as it was sometimes known, embraced much of what is now Dunellen. Therefore, it seems reasonable to assume that the road did in fact continue north of the tracks of the Central of New Jersey Railroad, on about the path of present day Main Street to and through to the west end of that community, then through present-day Middlesex Borough to Bound Brook.

Before leaving Plainfield, however, let us stop for a bit and see the Friends Meeting House on Watchung Avenue which was built in 1788. We should also visit the Nathaniel Drake House, now a museum, on West Front Street, which

Friends Meetinghouse in Plainfield.

Duncan Phyfe House near Dunellen, now used as a church school.

was used by Washington as a meeting place with his scouts and spies.

As in the vicinity of Elizabeth, our original road here is lost in the network of present streets and highways so it is necessary to drive on to Dunellen. Before continuing through Dunellen we should turn left and drive down New Market Road to see the Duncan Phyfe House. This beautiful building in the Classic Revival style, with its imposing columns, is one of the finest buildings of that architectural style in the country. Duncan Phyfe, the world-renowned furniture craftsman, built the house for his daughter Eliza in 1814. Phyfe was famous as a cabinetmaker and his early nineteenth-century work was influenced by French Empire style and the designs of Sheraton and of Hope. We well remember, many

93

years ago, his workshop in the rear of the house and, when we last saw it shavings still covered the floor. They were possibly the last he made before his death.

A left turn at the west end of Dunellen will take us to and through the village of Lincoln, a part of Middlesex Borough. The main street and highway to Bound Brook follows approximately the original route of the Old York Road. Crossing the Bound Brook, which is the eastern boundary line of the borough, we are again in a community with a great historic heritage. Bound Brook was, in fact, the first settlement in Somerset County.

At the eastern end of the borough a left turn through the railroad underpass brings us to a piece of the original Old York Road. Near the Raritan River and between the tracks of the Lehigh Valley and the Central of New Jersey is an old stone bridge that dates back to the seventeenth century. It was to the east of this bridge that the Old York Road left the King's Highway it had followed from the forks of the Raritan, and continued north and east to its terminous at Elizabethtown. The tracks of the Central Railroad of New Jersey were laid near the route of our road from Bound Brook west to Somerville.

The first house in Bound Brook was erected in 1683 by Thomas Codrington. The house, of which no trace remains, was built on an elevated site said to have been an Indian burying ground, and this is the origin of the legend that the house was haunted. So strong was this belief, during the early years of the dwelling, that the servants dared not go out alone at night for fear they would be carried away by an Indian ghost. The house stood for over one hundred and seventy years until it was torn down in 1854. It was known as "Racawachanna," an Indian name meaning, "the loamy flats by the running brook."

Near the Middlebrook, the west boundary of the borough, formerly stood the Fisher Tavern. It is said that the first Masonic Lodge in Somerset County was organized here. Whether or not that is true, it is a fact that General Washington did attend Masonic meetings in the Tavern, which was a favorite of both officers and enlisted men of the Continental Army.

On the south face of First Watchung Mountain is Camp Middlebrook. According to tradition, the thirteen-star flag, reputedly made by Betsy Ross of Philadelphia, was first raised over American troops there. Even the Washington Camp Ground Association, which in 1889 dedicated the site as a historic memorial, believed the story about the flag, as is indicated on a plaque at the Camp Ground, which is inscribed, "On this spot the stars and stripes were first unfurled over the Continental Army after their official adoption by Congress June 14, 1777. By authority of Congress the Betsy Ross flag flies here twenty-four hours a day."

We are reluctant to admit that our cherished beliefs over the years about the flag must be drastically revised in the interest of historical accuracy.

On June 14, 1777, Congress did in fact pass the resolution: RESOLVED: that the flag of the United States be made of thirteen stripes, alternate red and white; that the union be thirteen stars, white in a blue field, representing a new constellation. However, further research has not uncovered any evidence that the so-called Betsy Ross flag was delivered to General Washington at Camp Middlebrook, or, in fact, that Betsy Ross made such a flag during the time the Army was at Middlebrook.

For those who would like to separate the myths from the facts about our flag we would recommend the reading of a recent book, *The History of the United States Flag,* by Milo M. Quaife, Melvin J. Weig, and Roy E. Appleman.

Just west of the Middlebrook still stands the Philip Van Horn Mansion. During the Revolution this beautiful Colonial house, with its long lane leading down to the Old York Road, was a New Jersey landmark. Its one-time beauty gradually deteriorated and it seemed that this lovely reminder of Colonial times was likely to become a complete ruin. However, the American Cyanamid Company, the present owner of the property, has restored the house and it is now used as an employees' club.

Few of the eighteenth-century houses have a more interesting background than does "Phil's Hill," or "Convivial Hall," as the Van Horn House was better known. During the Revolution, Van Horn, whose sympathies were with the Crown, remained a neutral during the war, and he entertained both British and American officers lavishly. His five lovely daughteres were perhaps among the main attractions to the officers of both armies. Two of the daughters later married American officers.

Many interesting stories have been told over the years about this famous place. One is that General Richard Henry Lee, known as Light Horse Harry, during one of the entertainments, rode his horse through the wide entrance hall and up the grand stairway to the second floor. Convivial Hall, indeed! There is another story that seems hard to believe about Lord Cornwallis and General Benjamin Lincoln of the Continentals. It is said that on the morning of the battle of Bound Brook, April 13, 1777, Lord Cornwallis had breakfast in the Van Horn House and that having withdrawn his forces and hidden in the nearby woods all day, General Lincoln of the American Army enjoyed dinner there.

Continuing west over the Bound Brook-Somerville road from the Van Horn house about two miles, a left turn is made to visit the site of the old Dutch Church, which was burned by Colonel John Graves Simcoe's raiders. Just before reaching the Raritan River a state marker tells of the former church location and, across the road and a few hundred yards in from the road, may be found the Van Veghten House, on a bluff above the Raritan. This charming old house, built near the beginning of the eighteenth century, is occupied by a tenant farmer, one of many who have tilled this land for over two hundred years. The house was old when the Old York Road first passed it. Washington and

The Van Veghten House at Finderne, General Nathanael Greene's headquarters during the Middlebrook encampment.

his army marched by on their way from their victory at Princeton in January to winter quarters at Morristown.

It was here that the famous Christmas party, given by General and Mrs. Greene for General and Mrs. Washington, was held. At this party Alexander Hamilton met the lovely Betsy Schuyler whom he later married at her home in Morristown.

To stand today near this venerable place, particularly on a quiet spring or summer day, viewing the wide sweep of the Raritan to the west and to the east, and the beautiful countryside around it, one finds it easy to understand why the Dutch settlers, who had come to the Raritan Valley from as far away as Albany, called this valley "the pleasantest and best inhabited land that man can behold."

Returning to the Bound Brook-Somerville road, we next enter Somerville and the first place of interest is the modern Somerset Hotel on the right side of Main Street. The present-day structure is on the former location of the famous stage stop that was known as Tunison's Tavern. Some authorities believe that part of the original tavern is incorporated within the present building. Tunison's was considered one of the best between the Hudson and the Delaware. Like most taverns of its time, it was a popular meeting place for local residents who frequented the place to get news of other places from the travelers over the stage road.

There was an earlier tavern than Tunison's that formerly stood at the forks of the road at the western end of the town, which at that time was called Raritan. The stages of the Swift-Sure Line regularly stopped there.

All of what is now the two communities of Raritan and Somerville was, until the beginning of the nineteenth century, known as Raritan. When the county seat was moved there from Millstone in 1814, the borough of Somerville was created.

From an advertisement that appeared in the Somerset County *Messenger* in 1826, the town was described as follows: "The village of Somerville combines many advantages. It is central, healthy, pleasant and easy of access. The Swift-Sure stage from New York to Philadelphia passes through three times a week, and a stage connecting itself with a line of stages and steamboats at New Brunswick, leaves the village every morning for that city and returns in the afternoon."

Our route continues along Main Street and under the railroad underpass. A left turn on Middagh Street takes us to the Old Dutch Parsonage and just beyond is the Wallace House, or Washington's Headquarters as it is better known. George and Martha Washington lived in this house and used it as a military headquarters on several occasions during the years 1778-79. It was here that Washington planned the strategy for the Indian campaign, that, successfully executed under Generals John Sullivan and James Clinton, broke the power of the Iroquois, the Six Nations who were the powerful British allies.

The Headquarters, formerly owned by the Revolutionary Memorial Society and now maintained as a historic site by the State of New Jersey, is open to the public for a very small fee.

Many of the original furnishings have been returned and one piece especially, a rare grandfather's clock which stands on the stair landing, has an interesting history. At one time when the village was threatened by the British, the works of the clock were sealed in a waterproof box and buried in the nearby river. The clock is at least two hundred years old and still keeps good time. On the second floor is a nine-foot box

99

that was General Washington's personal trunk which, when traveling, was placed on a wheeled carrier and pulled along the road by a mule.

During the occupation of the house by the Washingtons many of the General's aides and officers were frequent visitors and overnight guests. Among them were the Marquis de Lafayette, William Colfax, General Sullivan, Lord Stirling, and many others. Conrad Alexandre Gérard, the first ambassador of France to the American Colonies, was also a guest on several occasions.

It is said that the Wallace House was selected as a headquarters because of its convenience to Camp Middlebrook and to the quarters of many of the high-ranking officers who met with the General to discuss plans and strategy. General Greene was quartered at the Van Veghten house at Finderne, Baron von Steuben at the Staats House at South Bound Brook. Other staff officers within a few miles' radius could be quickly notified of meetings by the fast-riding couriers who were constantly on the Old York Road.

Across the street from the Headquarters is the Old Dutch Parsonage, which was built by the Reverend John Frelinghuysen in 1751. He and his family were among the earliest of the Dutch settlers in the valley. Ministers, statesmen, and military officers have added to the luster of this family over the years, and descendants of the Reverend John are still contributing to the public service in Congress and in other important offices.

The Parsonage is now owned by the local chapter of the Daughters of the American Revolution who maintain it as a museum, open to the public at certain hours. It was in this building that the first theological seminary of the Dutch

Reformed Church was instituted. This later became Rutgers College, now Rutgers, The State University.

Adjoining Somerville on the west is the borough of Raritan and it is west of this community that a journey over the Old York Road will be most rewarding. Except for some new houses, the countryside appears much as it has for the past century. In fact, it was only twenty-five or so years ago that much of our road west of the Raritan was a high-crowned dirt road, as it had been since it was opened in 1764.

At the west end of the town there is a monument commemorating the friendly relations with the Indians that made possible the widening of the Indian path into the Kings Highway which later became a part of the Old York Road.

To the left of the road, as one travels west, is the canal originally built to supply power for the turbines that generated electricity for the fabulous James B. Duke estate across the river. The canal and the land as far as the juncture of the South and North Branches of the Raritan is now a part of the Somerset County park system. The Indian name for the meeting place of the North and South Branch rivers was "Tucca-Ramma-Hacking" which meant the "meeting place of the waters."

The early settlers of the Raritan Valley were mainly the Dutch from New York City, Long Island, and, in fact, from as far away as Albany. They drove their great wagons, piled high with all their worldly goods, over the Old Dutch Road from Elizabethtown to New Brunswick and then up the Kings Highway to Bound Brook and on to the forks of the river.

The wagons, drawn by four and sometimes six draft horses, with the Dutch families dressed in their quaint costumes, created a great deal of interest as they passed along the road.

Tunison's Tavern in Somerville was a favorite overnight stop, and in the evening the travelers from New York would visit there with the local people to exchange news for suggestions as to the best places to settle. They conversed in the common language, Dutch, as English was seldom heard in the valley during those early days.

What were the thoughts of those sturdy Dutch people as they made their way slowly through the Raritan Valley? We cannot know, of course, but we can understand something of their joy and satisfaction in knowing that soon they would establish a home in the lush and lovely valley, on land as fertile as any they had known in the old country.

The Raritan River, the name of which was derived from the Indian designation "Laleton," meaning "forked river," ran through the heart of the valley and provided a plentiful supply of water for the cattle and the many grist mills that were built along its shores. The Dutch soon learned, as the Indians had known for centuries, that the spring freshets deposited a new layer of rich river loam on the meadows each year. Bountiful crops were harvested on the meadows. The grains were later ground in the nearby mills and the flour floated down river in flatboats to tidewater at what is now Landing Bridge, above New Brunswick.

As far back as 1683, Thomas Rudyard, in his book on the American Colonies, mentioned the Raritan as a river that would probably assume large importance in the commerce of the Colonies. Peter Kalm, a visiting Swedish scholar, in his book of impressions of this country, said that the Raritan would one day be the chief waterway in America. He was right at least in his prediction of the importance of the river to the economy of New Jersey.

In 1806, John Davis, an English poet, described this lovely
stream in his "Ode to the Raritan, Queen of Rivers":

> All thy wat'ry face
> Reflected with a purer grace,
> Thy many turnings through the trees,
> Thy bitter journey to the seas,
> Thou queen of Rivers, Raritan.

The great movement to settle the Raritan Valley during
the latter part of the seventeenth century and the early years
of the eighteenth century was partly a result of the publica-
tion of an enthusiastic report made public in Holland by
Cornelius van Tierhoven about the farming possibilities of
the valley. He reported that the district was inhabited by a
nation called the "Raritangs" who lived on a fresh-water
stream that flowed through the center of a lowland which
the Indians cultivated. As most of the state was forested, the
meadows appealed to the Dutch because it would be easy to
farm them without the labor of clearing the land of trees
as was necessary with most interior land tracts.

From the forks west to the Delaware the lovely rolling
countryside of Somerset and Hunterdon Counties and the
many eighteenth-century buildings, most of which have been
standing since, and in many cases, before the Old York Road
was opened, are vivid reminders of an earlier day and a sim-
pler way of life. Side roads with names like "Barley" and
"Wheat Sheaf" add to the charm of this part of the road.
From this point west to the Delaware, and in fact all the way
to Philadelphia, one sees the street and highway signs reading "Old York Road."

From the forks the present-day road follows very closely

The blacksmith shop at Centerville, believed to have been built during the latter part of the eighteenth century.

the route of the original road, except where bends have been straightened out. It runs due west with a sharp left turn at a point near Readington, which during the earlier days was known as Readings. To follow the road to Centerville the modern Highway 202 is crossed twice. It is only a few miles to this lovely village, little changed from the days when it was the overnight stop on the stage road between New York and Philadelphia. It is a place that one should not hurry through. The tavern, for many years the overnight stop, was burned down but much of the original horse barn is still standing. It is now a community center. The center of the village is a crossroads, with the old store on one corner and the site of the former tavern on another. The old blacksmith shop is across the road from the store and is now used as a private garage. Not far west of the store, now a private residence, is a tiny building that was a barber shop many years ago.

The most interesting building is of course the barn where the relief horses were stabled during the days of the stage-coach. There is some question as to just how much of the present building is original but it appears that most of the timber frame is. The siding, which was originally plain barn boards, has been covered with shingles to keep the weather out and make possible the use of the barn for community affairs.

No more, as it was stated in a vivid description in "Two-Hundred and Fifty Years of Somerset," can "the blare of a coach horn be heard a half mile away, as the east- or west-bound coach approached the village of Centerville. The four or six horses a-lather and the green and gold coach flashing and swaying as it came round the bend was a wonderful sight to behold. The coachman, riding aloft, resplendent in buckskin breeches, top boots, red vest, and gold-banded silk hat. With the driver cracking his whip, the stage would swing into the inn yard with a flourish."

The present-day residents of Centerville have a deep sense of history and they are proud that their village remains a quiet oasis in the turbulent and uncertain world of today. Fortunately, the modern highway is far enough away to di-vert most of the motor traffic. We sincerely hope that the quiet charm of this little village will endure for a long time to come.

The small stream that runs through the village was the site of former Indian villages. Many evidences of their earlier occupation have been found along its banks.

There are few villages like Centerville left today. Here and there in some parts of New England one may still be found. The authors find such places a source of renewal, and in them feel the pull of events of an earlier day. It is good to feel such things, we believe, when so many changes are taking place in the world around us. When visiting Centerville, particularly on a quiet summer day, as we have done so many times, stop a while and just listen. One can almost believe that the horn of an approaching stage can be heard.

Three Bridges, a few miles west of Centerville, is still the quiet little hamlet it has always been and a few miles beyond is Reaville where our road meets the Amwell Road to New Brunswick. The Old York Road makes a sharp right turn and continues west to Larison's Corner, or Pleasant Corners as it was also known.

When the Swift-Sure Stage Line first opened for business between Philadelphia and Elizabethtown Point in 1769 it followed the Old York Road between Three Bridges, Reaville, and Ringoes. However, at around the beginning of the nineteenth century the stage route was shifted from the Old York Road at Ringoes and continued to Flemington for the overnight stop. From that point it continued to Centerville. We shall, in our journey, follow the original route.

From Reaville the road runs along a high ridge and the beautiful countryside is visible for miles. As Larison's Corner is reached, the village church is on the left with the cemetery across the road. Here are buried several generations of the early settlers of the area, who for the most part were of German ancestry. Across from the cemetery formerly stood Larison's Tavern, described in detail earlier in these pages.

Just west of Larison's Corner is Ringoes, which was settled about 1721. This was a very important community dur-

Larison's Corner Church, built in 1817, replaced a previous structure built in 1749. In the present congregation are many descendants of early settlers of the area.

ing the days of the first settlement of the Amwell Valley, with the village the trading center for miles around.

In the center of the village still stands the Jersey sandstone building that was the Amwell Academy, but which is now unfortunately a package store. The Academy was not built until 1811 and when it opened it became very popular as an educational institution, attracting students from as far away as Baltimore.

Beyond the Academy on the left side of the road is the Landis house, believed to be one of the oldest standing buildings in Hunterdon County. It was here that Major General

Amwell Academy at Ringoes.

the Marquis de Lafayette was brought from Valley Forge
by a local doctor to recuperate from an illness. The house is
often referred to as the Lafayette House. The original beauty
of the sandstone walls of this Dutch architecture has been
hidden with plaster, and concrete columns now adorn the
front porch.

Ringoes has an interesting history dating back to the first
land purchase near the beginning of the eighteenth century.
The first building was a log tavern, also used as a residence,
at the junction of the roads to Lambertville, then known as
Coryell's Ferry and present-day Route 69, a former Indian
path to Trenton. The latter was described as "one running
north and south, being the path of the Minsie Indians, from

Muskanecum Hills to the wigwams of the Assunpinks [Trenton]." The Lambertville road was the "great east and west path" (the Naraticong Indian path) which was later to become a part of the Old York Road.

Soon after Ringo built his cabin tavern, other settlers bought land in the valley and built their homes. Many of those early houses are still occupied by the descendants of the first settlers. One of the oldest houses is that built by Peter Fisher on land he purchased in 1729. His first home was a log cabin and the present house was not built until 1741.

Peter Fisher and his friend Peter Johann Rockefeller came to this country on a sailing ship from Germany. Their ship was bound for New York but was blown off course and landed its passengers in Philadelphia. Peter Fisher and his

The Landis House at Ringoes as it appeared during the nineteenth century.

The Peter Fisher homestead before restoration. It was built in 1741 with timber rafted down the Delaware.

friend walked up the Delaware Valley intending to walk overland to New York, their original destination, but when they saw the country of western Hunterdon they decided to settle there. Accordingly, they bought adjoining farms west of Ringoes and near Rocktown.

The authors owned, until a few years ago when it was stolen, the original deed to the land that was conveyed to Peter Fisher from Benjamin Field in 1729. The deed was also signed with the mark of Indian Chief Himhammoe.

Jacob Fisher, a grandson of Peter, built a stone house on the Old York Road a mile east of Lambertville, as it is known today. He was a blacksmith by trade and conducted a smithy in which he made axes, chisels, knives, and other implements that in that day could only be obtained from a blacksmith. Until the latter part of the eighteenth century there were no industrial establishments for the manufacture of such things as tools and implements.

Dr. C. W. Larison, who married one of the granddaughters of Peter Fisher, was a well-known figure in the field of education during the middle of the nineteenth century in Ringoes. He purchased the Amwell Academy about 1868. Among his many contributions was his efforts to establish phonetic spelling. In 1883 he wrote and published a book entitled "Fonic Speler and Sylabater" and on the title page of his book was the statement that it was "Desind As an Ad in Aquiring A Noleg Ov The Fundamental Principls Ov the English Lanwag."

The right fork of the road out of Ringoes to the west is the Old York Road. In one or two places the present road

Fireplace in the Fisher homestead.

leaves the original route; otherwise, Route 202 from Ringoes to Lambertville follows the same path as it did when it became the Old York Road in 1764.

On the right, a half-mile west of Ringoes is the Skillman House, generally known as the "Queen of the Valley." At either end of this impressive brick Colonial mansion are massive chimney breasts. In several of the rooms there are some of the finest examples of hand-carved fireplace mantles to be found anywhere. Some of the paneling is beautifully tinted from age and the wide floor boards are original. It is said that the brick of which the house was made was molded on the farm. The hand-carved dentil work under the eaves is exquisite. The cellar floor is paved with brick, as in many houses of that period, to provide a cool place for perishables.

The Skillman homestead on the Old York Road a mile southwest of Ringoes.

Former stage tavern at Mount Airy.

From this point the hills of the Delaware Valley are in sight. About half way to Lambertville the original route makes a wide swing to the left from the main road, and passes through the hamlet of Mt. Airy. In the center of the village still stands the old sandstone community building that was the Holcombe storehouse, built in the middle of the eighteenth century. It was a common storehouse for the farmers for miles around who stored their flax, grain, tallow, and other farm products until they could be carted over the road to Coryell's Ferry and floated down river in the Durham boats during the spring high water.

In view of the fact that there were very few roads other than the local "ways" in and between villages, those who were able to store their produce in the Mt. Airy storehouse were fortunate. The Delaware River was their highway to a good income.

Two of the early stage taverns are still standing in Mt. Airy. Both are now used as private residences. The old church and churchyard are interesting and worth a visit.

Just a short distance west of the village the old road again merges with the present highway. As the road drops into the town of Lambertville, one's sense of history is sharpened. A drive down along the river and a short walk enables the tourist to get a close look at the canal feeder and the old lock and locktender's house. The house is shaded in summer by huge old sycamore trees and the light and shadow effect on a sunny day makes the scene a favorite with artists and photographers. It is well worth seeing even though the lock gates no longer function. Concrete spillways now regulate the

The Delaware and Raritan Canal feeder below Lambertville.

A nineteenth-century picture of a canal barge at the lock on the Delaware and Raritan Canal feeder at Lambertville.

flow of the water. The feeder was built in 1832 to carry water from the Delaware River to the main Delaware and Raritan Canal at Trenton. In those days there was no mechanical earth-moving equipment and the feeder and the canal were built with pick, shovel, and horse-drawn drags. The labor for that tremendous job was largely drawn from the ranks of Irish immigrants. During the course of the construction, an epidemic of Asiatic cholera broke out, and many of the laborers who died from it were buried along the banks of the waterway.

The job was finally finished and both the feeder and the canal were ready for navigation in the summer of 1834. The water of the feeder, which flowed to the canal by gravity from

The home of James Marshall's parents on Bridge Street in Lambertville.

the higher elevation at the source in the Delaware, kept the forty-four miles of the canal from New Brunswick to Bordentown supplied with water, as it does the canal from Trenton to New Brunswick today.

Lambertville has many historic places. On the north side of Bridge Street stands the James Philip Marshall house. It was here in his father's house that James Wilson Marshall was born in 1810. Young Marshall was a carpenter and he worked his way west until he reached Kansas where he joined a wagon train bound for California. While building a sawmill on the American River, he was the first to discover gold, thus starting the famous gold rush of 1849. Marshall and his partner, General John Sutter, became famous but both died penniless.

Farther west on Bridge Street is the historic Lambertville House, built by Captain John Lambert in 1812, two years before the first covered bridge was built across the Delaware at that point. This quaint hostelry is little changed from the days when it first served travelers over the Old York Road, which passes its doors. Modern conveniences have been added but it still has the charm of an old inn. Jack Allen conducts the hotel as did earlier hosts and, for those who enjoy an overnight stop in an old inn and exceptionally good food, the Lambertville House is highly recommended by the authors, who have often been guests there.

In the churchyard of the nearby Presbyterian Church is the grave of George Coryell, the son of Emanuel who founded the village of Coryell's Ferry which is now Lambertville. On the marker over the grave is inscribed the following: "Here lies the body of George Coryell, who died February 18, 1851, aged ninety-one years." On the reverse

The Lambertville House, built in 1812, replaced an earlier stone tavern.

side is chiseled, "The last survivor of the six men who laid the Father of our Country in his tomb."

Up the road toward Stockton, near the north boundary of the village, is the Richard Holcombe House in which General Washington was a guest on two occasions.

While Lambertville does not seem to appeal to tourists as much as does her neighbor New Hope across the river, it is less hectic and the charm of its many historic sites, antique shops, book stores, and good places to dine may be more quietly enjoyed.

From Lambertville to Stockton and the country inland toward Flemington more and more people of the arts are settling as permanent residents. For the lover of antiques the whole area is a happy hunting ground. The summer stock season attracts thousands nightly to both the Bucks County Playhouse in New Hope and to the Music Circus on the hill above Lambertville.

James P. Snell in his *History of Hunterdon and Somerset Counties* said of Lambertville, "The hills immediately to the east and southeast of the town are quite bold and abrupt, but those to the northeast and north rise up with gentle acclivity. From these hills there are extensive and beautiful views of the surrounding country.

"From the most elevated points near the town may be seen the range of the Orange Mountain, nearly 30 miles away, Pickel's Mountain, near White House station, in the upper part of this county and distant about 25 miles, and, about the same distance to the northwest, the Haycock Mountain, in Pennsylvania. Few places have more picturesque surroundings than has Lambertville, and the wonder is that it has not attracted more of the attention of the lovers of fine scenery."

Since Snell wrote his description in 1880, many people have come to love the beauty of the hills and the river valley in the vicinity of Lambertville.

John Holcombe of Abington, Pennsylvania, purchased a large tract of land in this part of the province in 1705 when the entire area was a wilderness crossed only by a few Indian paths. One of those was a path from Neshaminy, in Pennsylvania, to the Indian encampments along the Raritan. The combination of heavy forest along the river and the river itself made this place a favorite haunt of fish and game. The last wolf was killed in this vicinity in 1880.

Many people still living remember the great shad runs up the Delaware River in former years. It is said that in a single day as many as twenty-five hundred shad would be caught by local fishermen. During the height of the run they were actually scooped up in bushel baskets.

Driving over the iron bridge to New Hope one may see on both sides of the river the former ferry landings which went out of business shortly after the first covered bridge was built.

Down the river a few miles, on the western shore, Bowman's Tower in Pennsylvania's Washington Crossing Park may be seen. It was the site of an important lookout during the Revolution and from it much of the Delaware Valley could be kept under observation.

Bucks County, Pennsylvania, attracts writers and artists generally. Some of the country's most famous are among the year-round residents there. They are naturally interested in the exceptional charm and beauty of the county. The facilities of Philadelphia are only an hour away and those of the New York City area are almost as close. Many from the county regularly commute to both those cities.

Today's visitor to New Hope finds a village where the atmosphere of an earlier century is combined with a bewildering array of shops, art exhibits, sculpture, and many similar places. The village is unique and travelers come from all over the country to visit and buy in the fascinating shops.

John Wells, the first settler, obtained a patent early in the eighteenth century on a grant of land of some one hundred acres to operate a ferry across the Delaware River. This was known as Wells' Ferry while the one across the river was called Coryell's Ferry. It must have been and is confusing as the name of Wells' Ferry was later changed to Coryell's Ferry. The community that rapidly grew up around the location of the early ferry, prospered as more and more mills were built on the little stream that entered the Delaware at that point.

The early ferryboats were small craft of many kinds. As early travel was on foot or on horseback, the passengers rode in the boat while the horse swam across the river behind it. Later, when wheeled vehicles came into general use, the ferries were larger, usually flatboats. They were equipped with hinged flaps at either end which, when lowered to the riverbank, enabled the driver to get his rig into the boat. Many early ferries were rowed and poled across the stream. Others, where it was possible to string a cable across from which the ferry was attached with a pulley arrangement, used the current as a means of propulsion.

Until a few years ago, on the upper reaches of the Delaware River, several of the larger, vehicle-carrying flatboat ferries were still being operated. A few miles above New Hope one of the cable ferries is still being used to carry a Jeep across to an island.

One of the most interesting places in New Hope is Logan's Inn, built by John Wells in 1727 to serve the growing settlement and the travelers over the Old York Road. Originally the road passed down Ferry Street to the Ferry Landing. Later, in 1814, when the first covered bridge was built across the river, the stage route was changed to what is now Bridge Street and that became a part of our stage road. The Inn was named for James Logan who was William Penn's secretary. In the yard of the inn stands a metal cutout of an Indian with bow extended. It was erected to honor Chief

Logan's Inn at New Hope was a convenient place to stop for refreshments before taking the ferry to Lambertville.

Wingohocking of a local tribe who were very friendly with the early settlers. Later the Chief took Logan's name as a gesture of eternal friendship. Sometime near the end of the eighteenth century the Chief and his family moved to the Ohio frontier. There some renegade whites murdered his entire family. From that day on Chief Wingohocking, who had been so friendly with the white people, turned against them and waged savage warfare until he died in 1790.

Diagonally across Ferry Street from Logan's Inn is the stone building, now a public library, that was originally where ferry tolls were collected. This charming old structure, built early in the eighteenth century, is worth visiting and is open during library hours. The ground floor fireplace, then the only source of heat, is still used, and on a winter day when a wood fire is burning the smell of wood smoke is pleasant indeed. A narrow flight of stairs leads to the second floor and the original hand-hewn beams are mellowed with age.

Directly across Main Street from the Toll House stands the mansion built in 1784 by Benjamin Parry. It required three years to build and was considered one of the finest Colonial homes in Bucks County. Parry owned a mill across the river in New Jersey known as "The Prime Hope Mill." When that was destroyed by fire in 1790, a new mill was constructed on the Pennsylvania side of the river, on the site of present day Bucks County Playhouse. This mill was called "The New Hope Mill." Thus the village that was originally Wells' Ferry became New Hope, as it is today.

According to the *Pennsylvania Gazetteer*, New Hope was, in 1832, the largest manufacturing center in Bucks County.

Stone house in New Hope built by Benjamin Parry in 1784.

Today tourism is the most important business of the community.

As one drives or walks along Ferry Street today, the many attractive old buildings on both sides of the street are evidence of the fact that New Hope is a very old community. In fact it is the oldest in Solebury Township. Its beginning was a land grant in 1710 from William Penn.

While Washington Crossing Park, which begins a mile or so south of New Hope, is not actually a part of the story of the Old York Road, it is tied to our highway through the events of history.

Malta Island in the Delaware at the southern end of New Hope, has lost its original identity. It is now just a sand spit.

Although a detour from the Old York Road, we urge our readers to drive down along the river on Pennsylvania Route 32 and enjoy the many interesting places in this lovely park. It is only a few miles to the Thompson-Neely House. Nearby are the famous wild-flower gardens of the park. For those who wish to lunch in historic surroundings there are plenty of picnic spots. The river views, the canal beside the road, and the flanking hills, particularly Bowman's Hill, and many other features make this short detour very much worth while.

To delve a bit into Revolutionary history, visit the David Library of the American Revolution in the Memorial Building. The librarian, Mr. William Holland, is always gracious and welcomes interested visitors. An impressive collection of maps and original letters written by George Washington and other famous people of the Revolution may be inspected.

Returning to New Hope there are many interesting things to do; good places to dine and to shop; in summer a ride on

One of the summer attractions at New Hope is an hour's trip on a mule-drawn barge along the Delaware Canal.

the mule-drawn canal barge, and the Bucks County Playhouse for an evening of the theater.

The jewel in the New Hope setting is the Delaware Canal which flows through the village. It was built in the middle of the nineteenth century to carry coal from the Lehigh area. The authors remember well the tiny coal barges that used the canal during the early part of this century. In fact, we could occasionally hitchhike on one of the string of barges and ride in our canoe without effort for a few miles. The bargeloads of coal destined for Philadelphia used the canal to its Delaware River terminous at Bristol. Those bound for New York were ferried across the Delaware above the wing dams and Wells' Falls and then continued down the canal feeder to the Delaware and Raritan Canal at Trenton. Coal was also carried by canal barge from Philipsburgh via the Morris and Essex Canal to the Hudson River at Jersey City.

The Delaware Canal, which is now a state park, is one of the loveliest recreational waterways in the country. As it passes through the countryside, it is today the setting not only for the older homes of an earlier century but many new ones. In New Hope, shops, homes and restaurants line its banks and add considerably to the charm of the village.

The authors, who have enjoyed the beauty of this waterway in many canoe journeys over the years, feel a special sense of gratitude to the members of the Delaware Valley Protective Association whose valiant efforts saved this historic waterway.

Those who have never seen a canal lock in operation may visit the restored lock at Lumberville. It is only seven miles north of New Hope. In the crisp fall weather a walk along

A lock on the Delaware Canal at Lumberville that has been restored to
operating condition.

the towpath is very worth while. While walking or for that matter, riding on the mule-drawn barge that is operated in the summer, the slow pace of travel gives one a better opportunity to contemplate the beauty and to recall the days of the operation of the canal.

Whether by car, canoe, mule barge, or walking, the entire canal is a joy to the artist and photographer with its mile after mile of beautiful scenery.

Driving west out of New Hope on Ferry Street our route merges with the present-day Pennsylvania Route 202, and follows it to a point just beyond the Solebury School on West Bridge Street. A street on the left, marked "The Old York Road," should be followed to continue the journey on the route of the original highway. This part of the road retains some of its original stone and plaster buildings and, at the point where Suggan Street crosses our road, a left turn takes the traveler to and across Aquetong Creek, on the bank of which may be seen the ruins of an early mill, now being restored. The mill was built by Richard Heath in 1702, and is believed to be the oldest one in Bucks County.

Returning to the Old York Road and turning left will enable the traveler to continue on the original route of the road for a few miles after which it again joins the present highway.

Among the many lovely pre-Revolutionary houses in this area is one that is known as Ingham Manor. Featured in Richard Pratt's *A Treasury of Early American Homes* it was described: "Built of what county people call 'tailored stone,' carefully cut and laid, its flat-arched windows and doorways, and its flanking wings at lower level, are signs of its pre-Revolutionary period, when stone houses began to replace the log cabins of the locality's earliest settlers." The

128

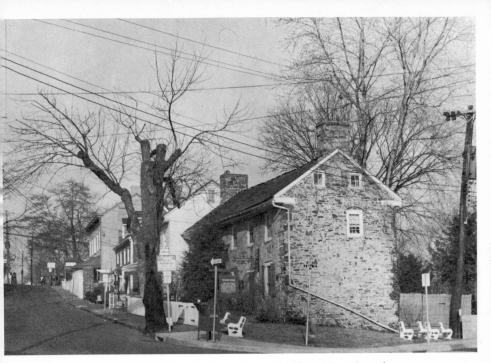

Many of the old houses on Mechanic Street in New Hope have been converted to a variety of interesting shops.

book describes what was known as "the walk-in fireplace," the wide opening supported by a massive lintel log of oak. A room such as this would have originally been the kitchen and the winter livingroom. The floor of Pennsylvania tile is typical, and the homespun Swedish table cover is set with country ironstone. It is altogether possible that the pine paneling of the livingroom at Ingham Manor is the work of shipwrights who settled along the Delaware in the early days, and who turned their hands to house carpentry when boat building was slow.

West of Indian Spring, halfway up the hill on the right, is another interesting house. It is called "Inghamdale," and was probably built during the early eighteenth century.

Inghamdale, one of the many eighteenth century houses along the
Pennsylvania section of the Old York Road.

Samuel D. Ingham, who was widely known as a statesman
and industrialist, was born there in 1779. He was Secretary
of the Treasury in Andrew Jackson's cabinet and held other
public offices. Ingham was a pioneer in the anthracite coal
industry and, as an ardent advocate of canals, was doubtless a
prime mover in the building of the Delaware Canal from
the Lehigh coal fields to Bristol.

Just east of Inghamdale, at Aquetong Cross Road, is a
pond of some sixteen acres that has been variously known
as "The Great Spring" and "Indian Spring." The Indians
knew it as "Aquetong," which meant "at the spring among
the bushes." Today, what appears to be a good-sized lake,
is actually a natural spring, said to be the largest between

Florida and Maine. It discharges over three million gallons of water a day. During the Colonial days it was the overflow from the spring that supplied the current in Aquetong Creek that turned the wheels of the many early mills along its banks.

Tedyuscung, the king of the Delaware Indians, was born near the spring and lived there with his braves. A rare degree of mutual respect existed between the white settlers and Tedyscung's people and they lived together in peace for many years.

Beyond the crossroad on the right may be seen another lovely stone house with an interesting history. It is the Paxton House, better known as "Rolling Green," built by Benjamin Paxton in 1748. During the Revolution, on several occasions, officers of the Continental Army were enter-

Aquetong, the Great Spring.

Rolling Green, where the Old York Road passes the Great Spring.

tained there. Like so many old houses, there are many stories of events said to have occurred in the place. One of those often-told tales was that on Christmas Eve, 1776, the night before the Delaware crossing, some Continental officers quartered in the house were cooking a Christmas meal of roast turkey and other traditional fixings. As they were about to enjoy the results of their efforts they received orders to march to the Delaware at McKonkey's Ferry. One can well imagine the disappointment of those officers but it is hoped that they received ample compensation in their glorious victory at Trenton two days later.

Just before entering Lahaska, one sees the buildings of Peddlers' Village a hundred yards in from the right side of the road. This complex of shops, including the Cock and Bull

An old-time carryall at the Maple Grove Farm.

Restaurant, is a recent York Road tourist stop-over, operated by two young and energetic people, Sheila and Earl Jamison. The country shop called the "Hentown Country Store" and over twenty more shops displaying all kinds of quality merchandise attract visitors from all over the country.

Descending the hill out of Lahaska, a beautiful view of the Buckingham Valley unfolds. It was from this valley that Chief Isaac Still led the thirty or more members of the Delaware Tribe on their journey west to the Wabash in 1775. That small band was the last of the Lenni-Lenape to leave Pennsylvania. As Chief Still expressed it when they left the valley, "we are going far from war and rum." That small band of a once large and powerful nation that had lived in the area for centuries left, it is said, with their heads held

The Old York Road has its share of modern shopping centers and tourist attractions, in addition to the many historic sites along the way.

high. Perhaps also in their minds was the following lament, author unknown:

> Where is my home—my forest home?
> The proud land of my sires?
> Where stands the wigwam of my tribe?
> Where gleam the Council fires?
> Where are my fathers' hallowed graves?
> My friends so light and gay?
> Gone, gone forever from my view,
> Great Spirit, can it be?

Buckingham Mountain, about two hundred and fifty feet in height and about a thousand acres in extent, was the haunt of a notorious band of outlaws during the Revolution, known as the Doan boys, presumably brothers. Like the legends of most bands of outlaws, the telling of their deeds became larger as the tales were told and retold. Wolf Rocks, on top of the mountain, is near their former hideout.

Before the Civil War, the mountain was an underground station that sheltered slaves making their way to the north. As this is written, plans are being made by the Bucks County Commissioners to make the area a county park.

Beyond the crossroad on the right is the Quaker Meeting House and School. The present building was erected in 1768. The original log meetinghouse was in the cemetery and was built at the beginning of the eighteenth century. The open carriage sheds, still in use, appear today as they did a century ago. On the porch of the meetinghouse and outside on the grounds are stone "mounting" or "horseblocks," as they were known, used by the Friends to mount their horses or to enter the high farm wagons in which the families drove to services.

135

One of the mounting blocks on the grounds of the Friends Meetinghouse at Lahaska.

During the Revolution the meetinghouse was used as a hospital. Many of the soldiers who died there are buried in "The Strangers Plot."

At the Buckingham crossroad is the General Greene Inn, originally Bogart's Tavern. It was renamed in honor of General Nathanael Greene whose headquarters were there for a time during the Revolution. The first meeting of the Bucks County Committee for Safety was held there on July 21, 1775. The wooden sign, adorned with the General's portrait, no longer hangs in front of the inn but it may be seen inside.

From Buckingham the change in elevation is noticeable as our road descends toward Neshaminy Creek.

A few miles beyond Neshaminy Creek our road enters

Hartsville, originally known as the Cross Roads. It is a quiet hamlet extending for a mile or more along the Old York Road. On the left is the Bothwell House or "Headquarters" as it is better known. This was the headquarters of General Washington from August 10th to the 23rd, 1777, and the entire army of between twelve and thirteen thousand men camped in the nearby fields. Here also the Marquis de Lafayette was sworn in by General Washington as an officer of the Continental Army. Like so many historically important places this famous house was for many years allowed to deteriorate, but restoration during recent years has once again made it an impressive Colonial landmark.

A short distance below the "Headquarters" is a private home that was at one time a tavern known as "The Golden Glow Inn." Originally a mill, the building still retains its charm. In our research we found much conflicting information. One source, perhaps with tongue in cheek, told us that the designation "golden glow" was derived from the fact that a few glasses of the liquid cheer served at the bar gave the patrons a golden glow. We doubted the accuracy of that source and were happy to learn later that the name was in fact derived from the mass of willow trees in the yard that make a golden glow against the skies. Despite the good volume of traffic on this part of the road, the entire length of the village always seems, at least on week days, an oasis of quiet so typical of this part of Bucks County.

In the center of the village the Old York Road is crossed by the Easton-Bristol road and its original name was "the Cross Roads." John Hart, who emigrated from Whitney in Oxfordshire, England, purchased a thousand acres of land from William Penn, half of which was in Warminster, in-

The former Golden Glow Tavern at Hartsville, now a private residence.

cluding the area that later became Cross Roads, later Hartsville. There is some confusion about when the first tavern
was built. It seems, however, that the village was named for
Colonel William Hart, the second son of James Hart of
Plumstead Township, who moved there sometime before
the middle of the eighteenth century. It is believed that the
first tavern may have been the little building on the right
side of the road that is now a gift shop. Other sources indicate
that the north end of the present tavern, the oldest part of
the building, was actually the first tavern. Whether the first
tavern was built by a Hart is not clear.

Cutting through a considerable amount of conflicting information, it is believed that John Baldwin was the first
owner in 1748 and probably he built the tavern. It was sold
successfully to James Vansant and Colonel William Hart

The Sign of the Hart at Hartsville was built to serve travelers over both
the York and Bristol Roads.

A state marker on the Old York Road commemorates one of the pioneer educational institutions of Colonial America.

who named it "The Sign of the Hart" or "The Sign of the Heart." The tavern sign had a human heart painted on it.

A state historic marker, down the road a short distance, marks the former site of the "Log College." Graduates of this humble establishment later founded many of our great American colleges. Founded in 1716 by the Reverend William Tennent, this early educational institution was housed in a log cabin. Among the great colleges that stemmed from the efforts of some of the graduates of the Log College were Princeton University, Dickenson College of Carlisle, The University of Pennsylvania, Washington University, and Hampden-Sidney College. Governor Martin of North Carolina, John Bayard, a Speaker of the House of Representatives, and many other illustrious men were among its graduates.

140

When the monument to the Log College was dedicated in 1889, the President of the United States, Benjamin Harrison, journeyed to Hartsville to participate in the ceremonies.

Beyond this point the former rural aspect of our road has been subjected to great changes. New shopping centers, a large parochial school and other modern buildings have been built. Warminster and Hatboro are practically one community now and both are growing rapidly as part of the Philadelphia suburban area.

In Hatboro is the old public library, believed to be the third oldest in Pennsylvania and the twelfth in the nation. It was founded in 1775 and in it today is a great repository of valuable source material for those interested in the history of Pennsylvania.

A Bucks County barn, typical of the early Pennsylvania farm buildings. The upper space was supported by stone foundations with tapered stone columns, providing implement storage at ground level.

In a small plot of ground on Jacksonville Road are buried the men who died in the battle of Crooked Billet. Near the end of the village is the former grist mill, the Pennypack Mill built in 1724, and now a favored restaurant.

The town of Hatboro was originally known as Billet. This was changed to Hatboro in 1740 and was so named in honor of John Dawson who came here from England to set up a hat factory.

On a pond not far from Hatboro, below Dansville, John Fitch conducted his early experiments in the invention of a steamboat in 1785 but his inability to raise capital forced him to abandon his plans. He did, however, successfully build and run steam-propelled craft on the Delaware River before giving up his dreams. Many years later, as every school child knows, Robert Fulton carried on his experiments, copied, it is believed, from Fitch and it was he, not Fitch,

The Hatboro Library.

Pennypack Mill in Hatboro was built in 1724, and named for a chief of the Lenni-Lenape Indians.

who received the credit for being the inventor of the steamboat.

It is still possible to follow the original route of the Old York Road through Willow Grove, Abington, Jenkinstown, and through Philadelphia as far as the Roosevelt Boulevard, but it is best to conclude a journey over this historic highway at Hatboro.

It is appropriate to close this narrative with a whimsical verse written at the close of the stagecoach era on our famous highway:

> And the old pike's left to die,
> The grass creeps o'er the flinty path,
> And the stealthy daisies steal,

Where once the stage horse, day by day
Lifted his iron heel.
And the old pike is left alone,
And the stages seek the plow;
We have circled the earth with an iron rail
And the steam king rules us now.

# Bibliography

The works listed herein speak eloquently of the help the authors have received from writers of an earlier day. A great deal of research has been necessary to gather the material for this book. To single out and personally and properly thank all the librarians and friends who have been so generous with their time and knowledge, or to acknowledge the diaries, newspapers, and other sources would be impossible. We extend our sincere thanks to the many who have been so helpful.

Battle, J. H., *History of Bucks County, Pennsylvania.* Philadelphia, A. Warner & Co., 1887.

Cawley, James S., *Historic New Jersey in Pictures.* Princeton, Princeton University Press.

Davis, Rev. T. E., *First Houses of Bound Brook.* Bound Brook, Washington Camp Ground Association, 1893.

Davis, W. W., *History of Bucks County, Pennsylvania.* Doylestown, 1876.

Farris, John T., *Old Trails and Roads in Pennsylvania.* Philadelphia, J. B. Lippincott Co., 1927.

Harrington, M. R., *The Indians of New Jersey.* New Brunswick, Rutgers University Press, 1963.

Hart, Val, *The Story of American Roads.* New York, William Sloane Associates, 1950.

Hoff, F. Wallace, *Two Hundred Miles on the Delaware.* Trenton, The Brandt Press, 1893.

Hotchkin, Rev. S. F., *The York Road Old and New.* Philadelphia, Binder & Kelly Co., 1892.

Kalm, Peter, *The America of 1750; Travels in North America,* ed. by A. B. Benson. New York, 1937; text of English version of 1770, revised from original Swedish.

Lane, Wheaton J., *From Indian Trail to Iron Horse.* Princeton, Princeton University Press, 1939.

Larison, Cornelius, *A Country Doctor.* Trenton, New Jersey Agricultural Society, 1953.

Lathrop, Elise, *Early American Inns and Taverns.* New York, Robert M. McBride Co., Inc., 1926.

MacReynolds, George, *Place Names in Bucks County, Pennsylvania.* Doylestown, Bucks County Historical Society, 1942.

Mellick, Andrew D., Jr., *Lesser Crossroads: The Story of an Old Farm,* ed. by Hubert G. Schmidt. New Brunswick, Rutgers University Press, 1948.

Messler, Rev. A., *First Things in Old Somerset.* Somerville, Somerville Publishing Company, 1899.

Mott, George S., "First Century of Hunterdon County" (paper read before the New Jersey Historical Society, Trenton, 1878).

Quaife, Milo M.; Weig, Melvin J.; Appleman, Roy E., *The History of the United States Flag.* New York, Harper & Brothers, 1961.

Quarrie, George, *Within a Jersey Circle.* Somerville, Unionist-Gazette Association, 1910.

Perry, Charlotte Stryker, *The Bucks County Scrapbook of Old Roads and Towns.* Doylestown, privately printed, 1948.

Petrie, Alfred G., *Lambertville, New Jersey, from the Beginning as Coryell's Ferry.* Lambertville, privately printed, 1949.

Pratt, Richard A., *A Treasury of Early American Homes.* New York, Whittlesey House-McGraw Hill Book Co., 1946.

Schmidt, Hubert G., *Rural Hunterdon.* New Brunswick, Rutgers University Press, 1945.

Snell, James P., *History of Hunterdon and Somerset Counties, New Jersey.* Philadelphia, Everts & Peck, 1881.

Van Sickle, Emogene, *The Old York Road and Its Stage Coach Days.* Flemington, N.J., D. H. Moreau, 1936, 1960.

Wildes, Harry Emerson, *The Delaware.* Rivers of America Series. New York, Rinehart and Company, 1940.